LIVING LIFE OFF THE GRID

THE STEP-BY-STEP COMPREHENSIVE GUIDE TO
LIVING OFF THE GRID

DAMIAN WALLAKER

CONTENTS

INTRODUCTION

"I took a walk in the woods and came out taller than the trees."

— *HENRY DAVID THOREAU*

Let me hit you with a few numbers... Across the expanse of this big, beautiful planet that we live on, over 1.7 billion people live off the grid. These people are living life to its fullest without depending on public utilities. They are connecting with Mother nature and using her fruits to be self-sufficient. Let's be clear here; these people are not living like cavemen like the common myth about off-the-grid living goes – not that

INTRODUCTION

there is anything wrong with such a lifestyle if that is your choosing. Instead, most of these people have opted to live in innovative, energy-efficient, inexpensive homes. Of this great number, a quarter of a million people have adopted this lifestyle in the US. The average cost of home ownership in the US is over $360,000 as of 2021, but buying a plot of acres of land and building a tiny home off-the-grid averages approximately $45,000. Is it any wonder that more and more people are choosing to live off the grid? And you can be one of these people.

Let's take a moment and picture you making that shift. Imagine if you could have a nice, clean meal every single day. One that is cooked with delicious veggies from your own farm. Imagine the satisfaction you would feel with every bite instead of suspecting what you eat in crowded restaurants, drive-throughs, and even what you get off grocery shelves.

The average household spends more than $2,200 every year on utility bills. Instead of handing over your hard-earned money for basic necessities, imagine having your own power supply system and never having to pay another cent for electricity. Imagine setting up a water collection source or sourcing water from a water source nature has provided. Imagine heating your home reliably without shaking your head over a bill.

Imagine the even sweeter satisfaction of resting our heads easy at night and waking up each day to the sweetness of a bird singing perched atop a century-old tree!

Do you feel my excitement because this sounds like a dream to me! If it does to you, too, off-the-grid living is for you.

If you are tired of city living and feel plagued by that lack of inner peace, then off-the-grid living is for you.

If you are tired of trading your health and happiness for pennies, off-the-grid living is for you.

If you are tired of the high and rising cost of cities filled with toxic industrial smoke, off-the-grid living is for you.

But I get it. You might have heard a lot about living off-grid and its benefits, but you are unsure whether it's a good option for you and your particular lifestyle needs. Perhaps you have already decided to live off-grid, but don't know how or where to make it your reality. Maybe, it's that you don't have too much money to spend on a luxurious homestead and are instead looking for affordable options and need advice. Or, you don't know about the best places to live off-grid and the legal, financial, and environmental factors of those places.

This book is the solution that takes away your pain no matter which one of the above circumstances fits why you have yet to shift into this sustainable way of living that brings you in touch with nature and gives you a great sense of achievement. Each page was constructed as part of a detailed guide on off-grid living that teaches how to adopt a more natural lifestyle powered by the optimal utilization of your resources.

From the ground up, you will learn how to plan, design, and build a modern home that allows you to leave a reduced carbon footprint on our planet while also being comfortable and happy. If your soul yearns for fresh sights and scenes, you will also get an insight into making a home on a trailer for easy travel. To top off your education, this book makes suggestions and gives guidance on securing food, water, and other essential supplies. We will do all of this on a budget. While transitioning to off-the-grid living requires an initial investment, you don't have to break the bank to do it either.

Becoming an off-gridder is not for the faint of heart, even though it is not as complicated as it seems. But it is entirely possible to achieve once you commit to educating yourself. My aim while writing this book is to give you the foundation that entices curiosity to know more. It is sad to say, but most people give up while trying to make this dream of off-grid living a reality because they are lost in what to do or which steps to take next. But the information I will reveal in these following pages will be your compass. This information is far too often obscure, but I will clarify it. No fluff and no filter. Just words that awaken you to the possibilities. That is my promise to you.

Stop slugging through a mundane life. Get ready to give your heart what it desires – A nest in nature where you are at peace.

Your future awaits. Turn the page to grasp it with both hands.

UNDERSTANDING OFF-GRID LIVING

The images posted on social media make us feel pressured to keep up. We are constantly bombarded with consumerism. We are stressed out by modern living, being overworked at jobs that underpay so that we can give away this hard-earned cash living in cities that are too expensive and do nothing to make our souls sing.

We need to remove the veil from our eyes and see the truth. That is not the way we are meant to live, surviving rather than thriving. We are killing ourselves this way. Instead, we need to take a step back and see what more life offers. Off-the-grid living is the lifestyle that gives you more. More peace of mind, more freedom, more space, more power.

What is off-grid living?

As opposed to what you may have heard, off-grid living doesn't mean living like a caveman. It does not mean you must give up modern conveniences or basic necessities. It certainly does not mean that we are stepping back on the evolutionary scale. Don't let misconceptions such as these scare you off from this lifestyle. So, if it is none of these things, what exactly does it mean to live off the grid?

To understand what it means to live off-the-grid, you first need to understand what the grid is. The grid refers to the electrical grid system from which we gain electricity in most modern settings, like cities. The most basic definition of living off-the-grid means living without mainstream electricity. Does that mean you must go without light and power in your home? It certainly does not. People who live off-the-grid opt to use renewable energy sources that facilitate sustainable living.

Turning to Google's search bar might mean that you come across other definitions that state that off-grid living is also synonymous with going without other utilities such as water, internet, sewer, and natural gas. I suppose this accounts for the idea that we must step back in time to live off the grid. However, this is not true. Off-grid living refers to only one utility, which is electricity. Everything else is customizable. Off-grid living means what you want it to mean. Therefore, living off-grid will be different for different people. It might mean living as far away from modern comforts as possible for some people. In contrast, it might mean simply disconnecting from the modern electricity grid while keeping all other utilities for another person. It might mean being self-reliant for food with having live-stock and acres of planted crops. In contrast, another person might have a simple kitchen garden supple-mented by trips to the local grocery. You choose the degree of self-sufficiency.

Entire communities are founded on people with similar ideas of off-the-grid living. For example, the Greater World Earthship Community of New Mexico is an over 600-acre development founded on the architectural style of building homes designed to act as passive solar panels while also serving as shelters. They are made from up-cycled and natural materials like tires and cans. Earthaven in North Carolina also uses alternative power sources, such as solar panels and hydropower. The Three Rivers Recreational Area of Oregon is a diverse mixture of shacks and vast homes powered by wind turbines and solar panels. This space serves mainly as a vacation home as most residents only live there part-time. This shows that you can have a hybrid of off and on-the-grid living.

As the examples above show, there is no hard and fast rule for off-grid living except that you disconnect from the electricity grid. You get to decide what it means for you. Therefore, the first step in becoming an off-gridder is to develop a vision of your life. Customize this to fit your needs and wants. From there, you can develop a plan for making this dream a reality.

Benefits of living off-the-grid

If you need some motivation to take the leap into off-the-grid living, here are some benefits that you will experience:

Reduced cost of living

Your monthly electricity bill will see a significant decrease as an off-gridder. Not only will your utility bills drop, but also the cost of living. You spend less money on obtaining land and square footage. Living expenses in rural spaces, such as groceries and entertainment are typically cheaper.

Freedom from dependence on the utility grid

We are using up our natural resources faster than they can replenish themselves. Climate change and unpredictable weather affect utilities and can cause unpredictable disruptions. There might come a day when utilities such as electricity and water are not as readily available as they are today. The self-sufficiency that off-the-grid living promotes allows you to be better prepared for that day if it comes around.

Home design choices

Often, we find that the homes in cities and suburban areas are carbon copies of each other. There is no room for creativity and uniqueness. However, off-the-grid living gives you more options in designing energy-efficient homes. You can recycle and reclaim materials to make a home that is just your style.

More space

Cities tend to be cramped spaces with people living on top of each other. However, off-the-grid living typically means a transition to areas where there is more square footage and acreage available. Populations are lower, so streets are empty, and stores and other facilities are less crowded. Off-the-grid living means you have more space to breathe, move, and live.

Increased proximity to and knowledge about the environment

Off-grid living promotes interaction with nature through activities such as hiking, climbing, fishing, foraging, and camping. Nature is typically right in your backyard, as all you must do is step out of your home to be in it. You learn more about the flora and fauna that occupies that space when you are in the thick of it. From that comes an appreciation for maintaining that environment.

Reduced carbon footprint

There are fewer cars and less traffic, so there is less air and noise pollution in rural areas. Light pollution is also reduced as there are fewer lights. We have grown more plants and trees, showing a marked improvement in the air quality. No matter how you look at it, such areas are better for reducing the carbon footprint we leave on this planet.

More privacy

Because you have more space to yourself, maybe even acres between you and your nearest neighbor, you can enjoy more privacy. You can play your music as loudly as you want, not worry about having people eavesdrop on your conversations, and even let it all hang out while you enjoy your living space.

Increased safety

The statistics show that crime rates are lower in rural areas because of a lower population. People in such areas know each other and thus, look out for each other, which increases safety. If you want to feel safer while you go for a run in the wee hours of the morning, let your kids play in the great outdoors, and enjoy everyday activities, then off-the-grid living is the way to go.

Is living off-grid sustainable?

People often use the terms 'living off the grid' and 'sustainability' together but living off-the-grid is not inherently environmentally friendly compared to living on the grid. How sustainable living off-the-grid is depends entirely dependent on the practices that you implement. For example, you may use solar power and have built your home with recycled material. Both practices help sustain the environment. However, suppose you are driving a gas-guzzling SUV with an engine that emits tons of exhaust. In that case, your energy consumption is not inherently better than someone else who might live in the city with a less energy-efficient home but who is driving an eco-friendly vehicle. If you rely on a wood stove or propane for cooking and heating off the grid, this is not more eco-friendly compared to someone who is living on the grid.

But as a point for off-the-grid living, the design of most of these homes is typically powered by energy sources like wind, hydro, and solar. They also have fewer energy needs, and they are better insulated. Homes such as those built in the Greater World Earthship

Community mainly used recycled materials during construction, and you can also go that route. These homes have these eco benefits because the designers and builders were conscientious about how these homes would affect the environment and they made sure to have a positive impact.

More practices that you can implement while living off-the-grid that allow you to be self-sufficient and have a good impact on the environment include:

- Using natural materials like clay, wood, and stone during construction.
- Constructing your home with energy-saving windows and doors.
- Turn waste into reusable items. For example, reusing tea bags and vegetable peelings as compost for growing organic plants.
- Recycling water. One such instance is reusing bath water to hydrate plants.
- Use energy-efficient appliances.

What is NOT off-the-grid living?

As mentioned at the beginning of this chapter, there are many myths, half-truths, and misconceptions wrapped around the notion of living off-grid. These can cause potential off-gridders, and even persons already in this lifestyle, to be put off the idea. My aim is to inspire as many people as possible to become self-sufficient by learning essential life skills that bring them closer to nature. One of these skills is living off-the-grid, and so I will arm you with the truth by debunking these myths and falsehoods.

Here are a few (and you should be on the lookout for others) of those wrong conceptions about off-grid living that you must never fall for:

You won't be able to earn a sustainable income

In this modern age, there are many possibilities for working online. You can even earn an income through entrepreneurship. Off-gridding does not limit your income potential. Not if you come into this with a plan and you can think fast on your feet, anyway. Depending on your location, you can even work part-time or full-time, in a nearby town. Where you settle may also offer money-making opportunities. For example, you can sell excess crops and items derived from livestock produced on your property.

You will see that living off-the-grid is typically much cheaper than city living and so monthly costs will decrease. You will not have to earn as high a monthly income to sustain yourself in such a case.

It will be hard to find gasoline

If you live in an area considered off-the -grid, you can still access gas stations and store what you need. The important thing to remember is that gasoline has a shelf life of (3 to 6 months) even if it is already in your vehicle's tank. Ensure that it's used within that time and restock as needed.

You're at risk in the wilderness

Most off-gridders live in homes within walking distance of their nearest neighbors. However, if you decide to be more isolated, you can learn to protect your home, your family, and yourself from intruders, accidents, and more. Taking a self-defense course, first aid, learning how to secure your home, and more are all handy skills that keep you safe no matter where you choose to settle.

You must own a large plot of land

You do not even have to own land to make your dream of living off-the-grid become a reality. Leasing and lending options do exist. Persons with free-spirited hearts do not stay in one location for very long. They do not want to be weighed down by land ownership, so they put their home on wheels so that they can travel at will.

You must be entirely self-sufficient

There is no rule book for off-the-grid living, and your dependence on conveniences such as a grocery store or local food market is entirely up to you. I know many off-gridders who find a happy medium between growing some of their own herbs, vegetables, and fruits while making weekly runs to the local supermarket for bulk buying.

Only farmers can be off-gridders

This is one of the most widely spread mistruths about living off the grid. While it is beneficial for you to learn farming and gardening skills, do not let this put you off from making the shift to off-gridding if these are not skills you already possess. Focus on the things that make you happy when becoming self-sufficient first. If you enjoy planting herbs, learn to do so instead of planting vegetables. If you enjoy planting fruits instead of veggies, then do that. Always keep in mind that off-gridding is customizable, and there is a wide range of pursuits that make it easier. Choose those that make you happy. Others can be developed at a pace that suits you.

Store solar kits will meet all your electricity needs

Store-bought solar kits typically come in the 45-watt version, but this will not power a typical home for even half a day. Suppose you plan to use solar energy to power your home. In that case, you need to put in that upfront investment, which is typically several thousand dollars, to develop a system that generates enough energy to meet your household's needs. Luckily, you may be able to subsidize this cost as many places offer incentives to purchase larger solar systems. The upfront cost might be heavy, but the solar panels last a very long time, and you can move them, or resell them if you no longer have use for them.

Doing laundry in a tub is a cinch

Anyone who believes this has not done laundry by hand. It is extremely tiring, especially when you have multiple people living in a household. That equates to lots of dirty clothes and many hours every week spent washing them. You also must account for drying time and whether the weather will permit your clothes to be dried at a particular time. Off-the-grid living is about living smarter, not harder. Consider buying an energy-efficient washer and dryer instead of washing by hand.

You should cover your roof with solar panels to gain solar power

This is not smart to do, as high temperatures can decrease the efficiency of solar cells. Rooftop solar power systems tend to get dirty with snow, leaves, dirt, bird waste, twigs, and more. It is quite a hazard to climb up there to clean up the mess.

Instead, get the more efficient option - ground-mounted solar panels. They are quick and easy to install, and easy to maintain.

You won't need propane

While your usage of propane is significantly decreased off the grid, expect to use it when solar panel units have no stored energy (such as times when it is rainy, and the sun is losing the battle with clouds) to get you through your energy needs.

Only if you have the highest quality solar power system can you get away without needing propane. However, the cost of this is higher than normal.

Wood stoves are a must for off-grid living

Wood stoves can be a hassle to use. Apart from the nostalgia factor, they are not all that is necessary for operating a household off the grid. There are several tasks involved with maintaining and operating them, such as collecting wood and maintaining the appliance. It is much easier to get a high-efficiency electrical or gas stove for regular use.

Chapter Summary

Off-the-grid living is about taking away the dependency on the typical electrical system and adopting a more sustainable and self-sufficient lifestyle that is closer to nature. Living off-the-grid is a highly personalized experience, and you can craft one that suits you, your ideals, your needs, and your wants. There are a variety of benefits, no matter what your personal vision is. Once you get past the myths and falsehoods surrounding this lifestyle, you will see that it is easier to achieve than ever before.

Living off-the-grid is not without its challenges, and the next chapter will supplement your education so you are adequately prepared to deal with them if they arise.

2

THE OFF-GRID CHALLENGES
(OVERVIEW)

*O*ff-grid living is all the rage these days. And why wouldn't it be with the many benefits it presents? A cleaner environment for us all. A lesser cost of living. The opportunity to reconnect with nature. I cannot recommend off-the-grid living enough. As with anything else in life, it's not all sunshine and rainbows out there in the wilderness; off-grid living has its challenges too. But knowing what they are allows you to be better prepared to overcome them. This chapter represents an overview of Off-Grid Challenges, and more detail will be put forth in future chapters.

The challenges of living off-grid

I have traveled to over 55 countries and captured some of the most awe-inspiring footage of the local flora and fauna. My goal is to visit every corner of the world and record as many natural places as possible on my GoPro. But that first trip? I looked cool on the outside, but on the inside, my stomach was tied in knots. And the first time I used my GoPro, I was afraid I would break the dang thing if I dared touch it too hard.

Those first experiences were nerve-wracking, and if I listened to the nagging voice in my head that said to give up, I would not have had all the wonderful experiences I have gained over the years, and I would not be writing this book for you.

You will likely feel like your nerves are being frayed as you step into this new world of experiences. But I beg you, don't give up on off-grid living. As with every new embarking, you will face some headwinds in those initial stages.

Some aspects of off-grid living that are commonly challenging:

Location

Location, location, location… It is not just a concern for suburbanites and city dwellers. Off-gridders need to be careful with this choice too. Where will you get the most bang for your buck when purchasing land? How much will you get, and what will you use it for?

Where is best suited to avoid the legal limitations of living without certain utilities? These and more are considerations when choosing a location that is right for you, and this can seem overwhelming.

Budgeting

Off-the-grid living does not automatically mean cheaper living compared to on-the-grid living. In the short term, you need to make a significant investment to take this process off the ground. But in the long haul, the potential for cheaper living is there if you make a budget and stick to it.

Power source

While living without electricity is an option, having power makes life easier. If you decide to obtain a power source, what are your needs and budget? Alternate energy sources need to be studied. In the area that you have chosen, what are the options? Even after you set up your energy source, you need to evaluate your usage and make adjustments to keep this consumption as low as possible.

Food sources

We all need to eat a balanced diet no matter where we live. Self-sufficiency should be the name of the aim when sourcing food as an off-gridder to ensure you get the nutrition you need. Learning skills like gardening, foraging, hunting, raising livestock, cooking, and preserving should be on your list of to-dos. You don't have to know it all when you first start this process, but it should be the aim to integrate as many self-reliant practices as possible.

Water supply

Water is life. It is impossible to live without it. You are not able to plant anything or raise any livestock without it. You cannot keep hydrated or clean without it. It is possible to locate land with a freshwater source, but if you cannot do this, it must be part of your plan to collect water and develop a running system. There are legalities surrounding the use of water even on your personal property, so you need to familiarize yourself with those for the location you have chosen.

Time management

Transitioning to an off-the-grid lifestyle is not an overnight process, and you need to manage your time wisely so that you establish the foundation for this shift while still maintaining the life you currently have. Also, after establishing your new home, you need to invest time in maintaining your home and up keeping the level of self-sufficiency that you have chosen.

Isolation and loneliness

Even introverts might find it difficult to adjust to the decrease in the level of human interaction after removing themselves from the hustle and bustle of city life. But isolation does not have to be your reality, even with fewer people condensing into a community. Choose a location that satisfies your need for socialization. If you prefer to go weeks without seeing another human being, then do it and choose a more isolated location if you can afford it. If you need some level of interaction, choose a location that suits it. You can find like-minded people in close-knit communities looking for the same things out of life that you are. You might also find that the skill sets of your neighbors combined with yours can set up a community of people that relies on each other to live comfortably at a lower cost.

The off-grid mindset

The best preparation for living off-grid is to prepare yourself mentally. Even the slightest inconvenience will throw you off course if you have not built the mental muscle necessary for this life. You are removing yourself from the normal conveniences and shouldering more of the burden of taking care of yourself. There is freedom in this, but there is also more responsibility. There will be lesser comforts and greater challenges as compared to what you see in the city, but it will be worth it if you are mentally prepared for the game.

Here are the qualities you need to build this mental muscle:

Tenacity

You might have heard this quality going by other names, such as determination, grit, and fortitude, but they all boil down to the same thing, hanging in there when the chips are down, and you are faced with a problem.

Adaptiveness

Life is a series of changes. In fact, the only constant that you can expect out of life is change. You need to be flexible and roll with the punches so that you can explore new avenues that improve your life as it changes.

Creativity

Humans were cold and going without hot meals, so they struck two stones together to create fire. We looked at the sky and decided we wanted to be like the birds, so we invented planes. We wanted to talk to each other even though the distance between us spanned miles and so people invented phones. Human beings have a knack for solving problems with ingenious inventions, and you need to harness that power within you and you become more self-sufficient as an off-gridder.

Positivity and mindfulness

Your attitude, no matter where you live, affects your morale. Learn to live in the here and now rather than ruminating on the past or worrying about the future. You will appreciate every minute this way. This appreciation leads to looking for the good things in life rather than focusing on the negatives. You will be all happier for it no matter what is going on.

Acceptance

Problems only grow bigger when we cannot accept them as they are. No matter how ugly or how disheartening, the first step to overcoming a problem of fixing a mistake is to accept it.

Looking on the brighter side

There is value in finding irony in even the most serious situations. Humor is a vital part of human survival. Use it to get through the challenges.

Engage in gardening and farming

Getting back to your roots always improves your mood and allows you to take on a more positive outlook on life. Even better is that there are entire communities surrounding these practices. You will feel a sense of homecoming and connection as you exchange ideas and learn more from other people like you.

Interact with wildlife

Science has found a direct link between a person's mental health and their level of interaction with nature. To feel happier, to increase your feelings of life satisfaction and to have a better mood every day, spend more time interacting with plants and animals. Stop to smell the roses. Watch the birds fly and sing. Cheer a caterpillar on as it crawls across a leaf. There is no shortage of ways that you can interact with nature.

The dos and don'ts of off-grid living

Knowing what to do and what not to do as you transition into off-the-grid living will significantly decrease your anxiety. Here is a quick list of practices you should do and others that you should avoid:

The dos

Get educated on off-grid living

The more you know before you make that move, the better prepared you will be for challenges.

Search for realistic locations

Where you choose to live off-the-grid determines your cost of living, as it is not just about the sights but also about the climate, the availability of land, land and property taxes, and building code requirements.

Study homestead possibilities

Based on where you have moved, uncover the options for your home. Will you be buying or building? If you are building, what type of materials are best to use, and what are the costs associated?

Investigate your energy and water options

Location also determines these. The size of your home and your usage also factor in your setup, the cost, labor, and the practicality of installation.

Ensure a proper source of food

Learn the practical skills that will make food supply easy. Is it a good idea to learn to hunt and fish in this area? What crops are best to plant? What plants can easily be foraged? What emergency supplies do you need, and what items are best to stock in your pantry?

Look into off-grid money-making options

Unless you are living off pension income or investments, you need to explore ways of making money when you live off the grid. Freelancing, gaining employment in nearby towns, selling handmade items, and more are options for earning this income.

Network with other people who live off-grid

Relying on others is always easier than trying to do everything by yourself. Integrate yourself into a community of other off-gridders so that you can share ideas and advice and ask for help when you need it.

Prepare a checklist before you launch yourself into the wilderness

I don't know about you, but there is something about a to-do list that gets me motivated to act. It also keeps you on track as to what you have done and what you need to do so that you are comfortably settled.

Take necessary precautions and safety measures

Just because the crime rate is lower in the rural areas where off-gridders tend to settle does not mean it is non-existent. Put measures in place to protect your home, your family, and yourself.

The dont's

Some of the mistakes that you want to avoid making while living off-the-grid include:

- Not installing a reliable power source
- Not having a reliable and safe water source
  Lacking gardening skills
- Not developing proper waste disposal

- Not developing your physical fitness so that you can cope with the physical demands of the wilderness
- Not understanding the costs Having unrealistic expectations Not having a support network

Chapter Summary

Everything in life has ups and downs and off-the-grid living is not exempt from that fact. Being new to the experience can make it seem like these challenges are insurmountable but with the right mindset - one where you are determined, adaptive, creative, and positive - you can make this work for you.

Next up, we will discuss the ethics of off-the-grid living.

3

ETHICAL OFF-GRID LIVING

orking overtime at jobs, we must drag ourselves out of bed to go to. Occupying apartments that are too expensive in overcrowded cities. Constantly comparing ourselves to the lavish lifestyles of online influencers only feels like we are falling short.

Modern life is stressful. It is a dark tunnel for too many of us, and it seems like there is no way out. But what if you could leave it all behind and live better? More peaceful with time to do the things you truly enjoy? What if you could reconnect with nature instead of being trapped in a concrete jungle? What if you could feel more achieved and accomplished with a positive impact on smaller communities? What if you could be more self-sufficient while you leave a lesser carbon footprint on the planet? What if you could connect with like-minded people who are just as tired of the rat race and want a slower, more relaxed life?

'What if' can become your reality with off-the-grid living. Empower yourself and stop depending on "the system". The first step to making this your everyday life is asking the right questions, especially since rumors make it hard to differentiate between fact and fiction.

The legalities

On top of that list of questions: Is it legal to live off-the-grid in the US?

The simple answer? Yes! It is absolutely legal to live off the grid. In fact, the American principle of personal freedom entitles you to that choice.

The more complicated answer? Yes, it is legal, but there are state tax laws and building codes you must adhere to if you want to live off-the-grid ethically and not land in trouble with the authorities. Such regulations include, foremost, land ownership. While it is possible to gain permission to occupy land or even rent land to live off the grid, my suggestion is to buy your own property and build your home if you can. However, far too often, many people squat on land that does not belong to them and even move into abandoned buildings, for whatever reason, thinking that it is their right to do so. It is not. Of course, this attracts the attention of authorities, and they are evacuated by the police. Do not let this happen to you. Give yourself peace of mind by starting this lifestyle on the right foot. You do not want to invest in this with all the other processes, like the installation of solar panels, only to be unceremoniously removed from the place where you rest your head.

Ignorance can land you in trouble with the law. Some times, it is the things that we do not know that throw a wrench into your plans. In that spirit, ensure you go over the deed for your land with a fine-tooth comb before you sign anything. Many off-gridders have been disheartened to learn after the fact that their deed restricts certain activities, like rearing certain types of livestock and even the number of livestock that can be kept.

Let me take a quick detour here... As we speak of live-stock, if you plan on selling raw milk from your off-the-grid dwelling...don't. This is illegal in most US states, and you will be arrested if caught. Some states allow the sale of "herd shares." In such cases, co-owners of livestock that produce milk, like cows or goats, can gain a pre-approved amount of milk from that animal for a return on that investment.

Back on topic... Owning a property means that you must pay property taxes. This applies even if you take off-the-grid living quite literally and you buy a remote piece of land. Taxes are subject to the regulation of each state. If you are trying to keep this payment as low as possible, buy property in states with lower fees. Hawaii has the lowest property tax rate at 0.3%. However, it also has home values on the higher end, so your tax bill can still be hefty. Alabama has low property tax rates and lower home prices, which might be more afford-able for some people.

Also, be aware that if you use your land to produce an income, such as with the production of produce and livestock, these activities are also subject to taxation. The IRS can make life difficult if taxes are not paid on time or in full.

If you have acquired a piece of land, you must consider housing. Camping is not a long-term option. You cannot legally do so for more than 2 weeks, even if you are the owner of the property. You cannot set up a structure on the land in any way you desire. Going that route will only lead to you getting fined or, in some cases, getting jailed.

You need to develop a house plan that the local housing authorities must approve. This plan must be developed in accordance with both national and international building codes. This is not the housing board trying to have fun at your expense. Instead, this keeps you and other people safe. As the building is constructed, it will also be inspected regularly to ensure the standard remains at each stage. To stay up to code, hire a building constructor who already knows the ins and outs or get caught up by reading The International Building Code.

Items you need to consider when building that permanent residence include minimum square footage. In most cases, this is between 500 and 1000 square feet. Approval of your home also depends on how you access water. Being connected to the water utility provider is the easiest option, but you can also dig a well or get that access through a natural spring if you are lucky enough to get a property with that. The collection of rainwater is something you can also consider, but not every state permits this. If you gain permission, making this safe for use and consumption is a must.

Energy production can also cause your building plan to be tossed out. You are free to produce your own electric energy. Residential solar panels. Wind turbines. Geothermal heat pumps. The options are varied. However, you need to be aware of the local restrictions to this production before footing the bill for the setup.

The great part about this is that once you are all set, you might be able to sell surplus energy to the local power provider.

Waste disposal is the last here, but not the least of your housing considerations. It is illegal to dump sewage in the environment as it causes harm to not only the plant and animal ecosystems there but eventually to humanity. Even off-gridders need to establish a sewer system for their homes. Even a composting toilet needs to be approved.

This is not a housing consideration but more of activities surrounding your location. Hunting and fishing permits must be obtained if you plan to make that part of your regular activities for supplying your household with food. This applies even if you are doing these activities on your land. Be mindful that some animals can only be hunted within certain seasons. Familiarize yourself with the hunting and fishing practices of the location. It goes without saying, but the illegal trafficking and killing of animals (poaching) is certainly a no-no. Off-grid living is partly about becoming one with nature. Robbing her of her resources, especially in such cruel ways, goes against that grain.

The initial cost of living off-grid

It's time to talk figures. How much is that initial invest-ment needed to make living off-the-grid a reality? If you plan on buying land, the first investment is gaining that property. It is possible to gain access to free plots of land, but those spaces come with tons of terms and conditions. You would still have to invest in making the land livable, so my advice is to put all that work and cost into something that has your name on it, if possi-ble. Most off-gridders purchase between 1 and 5 acres of land. This will cost between $20,000 and $30,000.

Other initial expenses include:

Shelter

If you have gained a plot of land without a home already constructed on it, you need to factor in the cost of erecting that structure. You have several options. If you hire a contractor, this typically costs between $120,000 and $150,000. A rammed earth house is a bit pricier at about $200,000.

If those are too steep for your budget, you can buy a simple pre-manufactured home for about $20,000 or a cabin, which costs about $50,000.

RVs are also an option, especially if you want to travel. A second-hand home on wheels runs you between $1,000 and $2,000.

Additional buildings

Other buildings you may choose to build and their average cost include:

- A barn to house livestock. This typically costs between $10,000 and $20,000 after including the building, installation of electricity and temperature controls, and the type of flooring and frame.
- A chicken coop to house chickens. A simple structure to hold 4 chickens costs about $150. The cost climbs with the addition of more chickens. More complicated models are around $1,500.
- A greenhouse to complete your food supply needs. Smaller greenhouses can be set up at a cost of around $750 while more elaborate setups cost approximately $10,000.
- A root cellar for food storage. Smaller sizes are about $100, while on the larger end, this can cost you around $1,000.

Power Systems

Wind turbines and solar panels are popular options for supplying off-the-grid homes with power. If your budget does not exceed operating a refrigerator, some options cost around $1,000.

The typical home needs about 5KW to power all appliances and provide light. Installing wind turbines or solar panels that will supply this need costs about $30,000 to purchase the equipment and install them. Batteries also need to be bought as a backup. Each battery costs between $200 and $300. Supplying the typical home requires about $7,000 worth of batteries.

Geothermal pump

This can be used as a cooling and heating system for your home. This works by extracting heat from fluids in the earth, concentrating it, and transferring it to the home to heat the home. The reverse happens for cooling the home.

The age of your home, the insulation quality that exists, its size, and more determine the price of the geothermal pump, so you need to ask a contractor for a quote to understand the exact cost of this.

Septic system

You may need a permit to install a septic system to get rid of human waste, so do your research for the chosen location. The installation of this system is relatively cheap, but this depends on several factors. Ask a contractor for a quote.

Composting toilets

These allow you to recycle human waste into fertilizer. You can DIY such a system for about $100 per toilet or install a centralized system that directs all the waste into one composter for more than $10,000. Asking a professional to step in has a starting cost of $1,900.

Well

If your land does not come with a freshwater supply like a lake or a stream, you may need to dig a well. The depth of this affects the costs as companies that provide well-digging services charge between $15 and $100 per foot. The average well depth is 100 feet. This runs you an average well-digging cost between $1,500 and $15,000. You do have the option of digging the well yourself, especially if you are digging several wells. This carries an investment of between $10,000 and $15,000 to purchase a drilling rig.

After they have dug the well, you will incur other costs, including the installation of a pump and plumbing and electrical work. Together, this can cost up to $2,000. Finally, you need water tanks for storage. The regular cost of this is between $500 and $1,000 per tank.

Gray water

Gray water is the runoff water from baths, sinks, washing machines, and more. This water is relatively clean and can be reused by installing a collection system. Reuses include flushing the toilet and watering plants. The exact cost of this depends on the complexity of the setup. As such, you need to get a quote from a contractor.

Gardening

To feed a family of 4 with all the veggies that growing boys and girls need to be strong and healthy, you need a garden that covers about 4,000 square feet. To grow crops in this area, you need to spend around $100 on seeds. Luckily, as the plants produce, this expense is removed since you can gather seeds from the plants. The exact plants you plant determine some cost as items like berries and nut plants can cost between $15 and $100.

Protect your plants from foraging animals with a wire fence, which foots a bill between $500 and $1,000.

An irrigation system may need to be set up depending on your garden size, but you can get by with the use of a hose.

Aquaponics

This is an aquaculture system where waste produced by the fish farmed in the ecosystem is used to provide nutrients for plants. You can gain both fish and veggies from such a system. The cost depends on the size. A small system costs about $500. To feed a family of 4 year-round, you need to spend at least $1,000.

Livestock

Common livestock and their associated costs include:

Chickens

It is best to get enough chickens to match the number of people living in your household, as each chicken lays enough eggs to feed one person. The cost of chicken is between $5 and $10. In addition, it takes about $2 monthly to feed each chicken.

Cows

One cow is enough to feed a family of 4 for 1 year. The breed determines the price. 1 cow costs between $1,000 and $3,000. Feeding this cow costs about $200 a month, but this cost can be lowered by using plants and scraps. Fencing to keep his cow safe and sound costs about $2,500.

You can earn income from this by selling the excess meat. The same is true for pigs.

Pigs

Between 1 and 2 pigs are required to feed a family of 4 for a year. It takes between $15 and $100 to purchase a pig. It costs about $3,000 to breed pigs. Feeding each pig costs around $50 but you can eliminate this cost by feeding the pigs plants or scraps. To house and fence, these animals cost about $500.

Routine expense

When your home is up and running, do not forget to factor in the cost of monthly living with items like food, fuel, travel, healthcare, repair and maintenance, internet, insurance, and taxes. The average cost for a family of 4 is about $1,000, but this is entirely dependent on the needs of your household.

Chapter Summary

While all states of the US allow off-the-grid living, laws and policies that govern how this is done. Such regulations include the payment of property and land taxes, power supply laws, water supply laws and building code and zoning restrictions. Defaulting or breaking these rules can get you fined and even jailed.

We have talked a lot about land ownership in this chapter. The next chapter delves deeper into the particulars of the activity.

4

PREPARING YOUR ABODE (OVERVIEW)

*O*nce you have the location where you will start your off-griding journey, the next consideration is what your humble abode will be like. What are the comforts that you just cannot live without? What are the things you need to make this experience the best of your life? Sometimes, we don't know what we can't live without until we are forced to live without them. This chapter was created to help you avoid that situation with a list of the most frequently used off-the-grid features that homes are outfitted with. Let's get you thinking about them before you design your home. Also, the following considerations allow you to develop a home with conservation of water and power in mind. This chapter also represents an overview of Preparing Your Adobe, and more detail will be put forth in future chapters.

KEY FEATURES of an off-grid home

Insulation

This is especially relevant for homes built in colder climates. Efficiently insulated homes conserve heat during winter and on cold nights. It also serves to prevent your home from heating up to quickly during summer.

Eaves

Eaves are the overhanging part of the roof. Incorporating them into your home design allows you to heat your home during the winter and cool it down during the summer. The dual benefit comes from the structure allowing the sun to penetrate your windows at a low angle during winter and preventing the sun's rays from penetrating the windows at a high angle during summer. This works best on the south side of a home that is in the Northern Hemisphere.

Solar panels

Speaking of the sun, solar panels are a popular way of gaining power by harnessing the power of the sun. As mentioned before, it is easier to install and maintain ground-mounted versions. It is best to angle these solar panels toward the south. This action allows for collecting the maximum amount of sunlight year-round.

Wood stove

These can make a great focal point in your off-the-grid home but using wood stoves is also an efficient way to heat your home during winter and on cold nights. For maximum efficiency, ensure that this is made of stone, as it allows the wood to burn for longer.

Heat recovery ventilator

Another way of conserving power by heating your home is the use of heat recovery ventilators. They transfer heat from stale hot air, leaving your home to the outside, and do the opposite of fresh colder air on the outside.

On-site electric generation

The one commonality with all off-the-grid homes is that they must be disconnected from the electric grid. If you plan on powering up your home, then you need to generate power on your own. Solar panels are one of the most popular ways of creating power right there on your property. However, there may be shortfalls in that supply, such as when there is cloudy weather or when winter comes around. Solar should not be your only means of gaining power. Explore alternatives, such as wind turbines and hydroelectric. It is best to develop a hybrid approach and have a backup to your main electric generation.

Power backup

Just like an on-the-grid home, it is best to keep your home powered up even when the main source of power is interrupted. One of the most reliable backup power supplies is propane generators. Propane generators are a better alternative to diesel-powered generators because they can be stored for longer without destabilizing. They are relatively cleaner-burning, and they give the user more versatile options.

Solar-powered indoor lights

Using LED lights in your home allows you to use about 75% less energy compared to using regular incandescent lighting. You can bring that consumption down to zero during the day by using solar-powered lights inside your home. These lights come in the form of clear tubes. They extend from your roof to light inside your home directly by harnessing sunlight.

Tankless water heaters

Traditional water heaters are tanks filled with hot water at all times. The maintenance of this heat is costly and not very green. Tankless water heaters allow you to enjoy the comfort and convenience of hot water without the tank. The water is only heated when it is running.

Up your conservation game by adding a solar water heater. Your water is heated for free while the sun shines!

Rainwater collection barrel

Many locations in the US allow for the collection of rainwater. The first thing that you must do to conserve water if you have chosen such a location for your off-grid home is to structure the roof with guttering that directs the water flow to strategic locations around the house. The next step is the collection of that water. You have several choices such as barrels and cisterns.

You can create a system that links to other barrels and cisterns and have the pump attach it and direct the water to where you need it. These systems should have screens built-in to keep out debris and insects. I also recommend installing a shut-off valve to prevent over-flowing and thus flooding.

Composting system

Here's an interesting fact: Wasted food contributes approximately 8% of greenhouse gas emissions. No matter how much you try to conserve food, the fact is that there are certain parts of food you're just not going to consume. Peels, eggshells, tea bags, and bones are examples. Most often, these unconsumed parts end up in landfills, but you can help protect the earth by composting such items instead. A simple composting system looks like this:

1. Select the food scraps. Fruit and veggie scraps are always a great choice. So too are coffee grounds, tea bags, eggs shells, and bread. Not everything passes the composting test, though. Do not add dairy, poultry, and meat products to this, as they will attract rodents.

2. Store the selected scraps until you're ready to compost them. You can use a simple sealable container. Place this in your kitchen to compile the compostable items. I like to store them in a freezer bag in my freezer so that they do not attract insects.

3. Create a place for your compost. The backyard is the most obvious choice to set up a compost bin, but if you do not have the space, you can also set this up in your living space, using the process of vermicomposting, which is inexpensive and takes up very little time and space. Earthworms are used to convert scrap

LIVING LIFE OFF THE GRID

materials into a hummus-like material called the vermin compost. All you need is an opaque plastic bin about 12 inches deep. Drill a few holes in the top and bottom edges of the bin and add a mesh screen. Finally, add dirt and worms. All that remains is the addition of the scraps.

4. Create a compost mix. This has two key ingredients: greens and browns. The greens are your food scraps. They release nitrogen and microorganisms as they decompose, both of which are needed to facilitate the process. The browns are carbon-rich ingredients like dried leaves, newspaper, and egg cartons. Shred them before adding them to the compost bin. They allow water and air to flow through the compost. They must be placed at the bottom of the greens.

5. Get your compost! Composting can take as little as 2 months if you're in a hot climate. On the other end of the stick, it can take about 6 months if you are in a cold climate. The more compost added to the bin, the faster the process will be.

Chapter Summary

To ensure that you are comfortable in your off-the-grid home, the feature you must consider even before you put pen to paper to plan its design include:

- Insulation
- Eaves
- Cisterns to collect water
- Solar panels
- Tankless water heaters
- Wood stove
- Heat recovery ventilator
- Power backup
- On-site electric generation
- Solar-powered indoor lights
- Rainwater collection barrel
- Composting system

With the primer of your off-the-grid home outlines, you can then move on to planning this home. We will cover this in the next chapter.

5

PLANNING YOUR OFF-GRID HOME

*W*e live in very hard times. The covid-19 pandemic and economic recession have made the cost-of-living skyrocket through the roof. Therefore, it is quite understandable if you might not have a huge cash flow to invest in living off the grid. This chapter dives into how you can plan your off-the-grid home on a tight budget.

Tips to build your off-grid home on a tight budget

Planning is the foundation of any successful project. Plan how you are going to spend your money down to the very last cent. Of course, things can come out of the woodwork, but you are better able to handle them once you know how you have allocated your funds for a building. This budget should even include a cash allocation that gives you some wiggle room for those unexpected expenses.

Look at the type of homes you would be interested in and how they arrange them. Educate yourself on the possibilities and costs of pursuing what you want. This research can lead you down a path that allows you to use alternatives that cost less and are just as good. However, I implore you not to look for shortcuts that cost you more down the line. Do things right upfront to avoid a headache later.

Next, consider the things that you will need to be self-sufficient. For example, you may love smoothies in the morning. Consider the cost and effort of growing a fruit and vegetable garden that accommodates the specific items you enjoy most.

Knowing your needs and wants allows you to budget and, therefore, work towards what you want. It may take a little time to save up if those finances are not already within your means, but you have a goal in mind, and that will be your compass for making your off-the-grid dreams come true.

One of the first things I always recommend to new off-gridders is investing in building a greenhouse. This is especially important if you live in a cold climate. Winter makes it almost impossible to grow anything outside but with a greenhouse, you can. Consider this the haven for your plants even if you live in a tropical climate. They protect your plants from foraging animals, insects, and extreme weather like sun exposure and torrential rains.

The cost of a greenhouse kit depends on the size, material used to construct it, and the additional features you chose, but these kits can be up there in price. You can build a greenhouse yourself to save some money. If you can recycle or repurpose, materials to build this, even better.

Take advantage of warmer periods to grow as much as you can. You might have to invest in buying seeds to start a garden, but you might remove this cost by asking neighbors for some of theirs and collecting seeds from foods you forage, buy, or have. Bought apples at the store? Don't throw out the core. Take out the seeds and allow them to dry so they can be planted. Later, you can get rid of this cost by saving seeds from previous gardens and allowing plants to reseed themselves.

As a side note, you can also grow fruits and veggies in containers if space is limited or if you cannot afford to invest in a greenhouse or garden right away. The first focus as an off-gridder should be surviving. Focus on gaining the things you need first. Once those things are in the bag, and you have processes that will ensure continuity, then you can focus on thriving where your wants take center stage.

While some of your plants might not be readily available in cold months, you can still enjoy them by learning to preserve foods. Canning and drying foods are just two of the options for food preservation.

Chickens are also a worthy investment I recommend, as they provide both meat and eggs. Buying the chickens is inexpensive. It is the maintenance that can pull in cost. But you can bring this right down with a little creativity and adaptiveness. Construct chicken coops with recycled or repurposed materials if buying them is too costly. Pallets are a popular choice for this. Many local businesses give them away for free. Research designs and have fun with the process. There are plenty of free designs to be found on the internet. Chicken feed is a recurring cost that you can also get rid of by feeding the chicken table scraps and veggies grown from your garden. Corn can be purchased on sale during deer hunting seasons. You can even shred their eggshell to infuse their diet with calcium. You can also get creative by feeding other types of animals cheaply without resorting to using store-bought feed.

Speaking of recycling and repurposing, the greenhouse and chicken coop are not the only structures that you can use up-cycled material to build. A friend of mine furnished his home entirely with flea market finds and reduced his bill by more than half, even after he invested in refurbishing some of the pieces. He gave these furniture pieces new life. They look great, and he has a few stories to tell surrounding them. When you take something apart, do not throw away the pieces. Store them neatly. You just might have use for them in the future. If you see someone throwing something you see value in, don't be afraid to ask for it. Salvage materials from construction sites; after you have gained permission, of course. Some of these items, like lumber, trimmers, and fittings, can be even used to outfit your home. If you want a home with character, this should be a serious consideration. There are even websites where you can purchase these reclaimed materials. Often, saving boils down to just being creative with what you alrcady have or giving something an alternative use. Think outside the box and that resourcefulness will take you further than any amount of money ever will.

Construction is a hard job, and building gets harder when you do not have the right tools. You can purchase brand-new ones, and I recommend doing so if you plan several projects. You can resell these after. But if you're strapped for cash, you can purchase used ones at discounted prices or you can call on a friend, family member, or neighbor to borrow theirs.

Sometimes, a project takes more than one pair of hands. This is another instance where you can lend a hand when needed and ask for one when you need it. Bartering of services and goods is part of a sustainable and conservative off-grid lifestyle. Not everyone is out to make a dollar from skills they have or items they stock. Some just want to help others. That can benefit you. Please do the same and help others without a fee when you can.

Often throwing money at a problem does not fix it. It is rather the mentality of the people involved that will get things done efficiently and productively. Having a tight budget does not deter you from living your dream off the grid. In fact, it might be the reason why you live this dream out to its fullest potential.

The off-grid architecture

Every plot of land is different, and so you need to assess the typography and location relative to other features to make the best and safest use of that property when building your home.

You need water to survive. This is a need and not a want. So, let's start with positioning your home accounting for this factor. Hopefully, you were able to gain access to land with a water source nearby or a well already dug in. Your home needs to be positioned in a way that neither of these poses a hazard while still making gaining that water as easy as possible.

If neither of these is the circumstance, don't fret. You can have a well dug up and gain running water by powering an electric pump with wind or solar-generated electricity. A hand pump is also an option, and I think you should keep one on hand in case your electric pump is not available for any variety of reasons.

Be sure that you always have water stored for emergencies as well. Your main water source, like a river or well, can become contaminated or dry up. Water can be stored in containers or barrels, but I recommend using water tanks. Pumps and pipes can be installed to make water delivery to your home easier. Plan how you will integrate this storage into your home design. If you plan to collect and use rainwater, this also needs to be figured into your design.

Apart from water sourcing, you also need to determine the sunny spots on this plot of land. These places are perfect for placing gardens. Once your survey of the land has determined this, note how easy it will be to get water to the location. Can a hose reach this area? Do you need to install sprinklers or a watering tank? Is it practical to do any of these things? If not, what is the second-best location for this?

You can get away with placing a garden on hilly spots on the land, but flat land is the cheapest way to go when it comes to building structures like your home, barns, storage sheds, and greenhouses. Otherwise, you need to put infrastructure like retaining walls and pillars in place to make these structures safe for use. Again, you need to factor in how easy it will be to get water to the locations. The cost can rise quickly if the land is not flat.

You have settled on your water source, where you will plant your garden, and where your house and other structures will be placed on the land, so it is time to figure out where to pasture any livestock you take on. Larger plots of land allow for pasturing animals more comfortably, but even if you have a small plot of land, all you need to do is ensure that the animals have enough space to roam. Larger livestock like cows should be placed further away from your home because of the odors they give off and because they are less likely to be preyed on by predators. Smaller livestock such as sheep, goats, and chickens can be placed nearer to your house as lights from the house deter predators that pick on smaller animals. The space that you pasture these animals does not have to be flat or piled high with grass.

LIVING LIFE OFF THE GRID

You may have to clear away a few trees from the areas outlined above. Depending on the type of trees, lumber may be used to construct your home and other buildings. The wood can also be used to create fences or as firewood. The trees on your property may be a valuable resource if you are creative enough to utilize them as such.

Fencing the parameter of your property can stop predators from picking off your livestock. Fences also keep livestock safe and at home instead of roaming onto other properties. They also make it harder for other types of unwanted guests, namely human intruders, from making their way onto your property. Parameter fences can be quite costly to erect, so this may be added later down the line.

Fences are a great way to give yourself privacy from wandering eyes. Strategically placing trees and shrubs also serve this purpose besides creating a natural fence. They are not expensive to put in place. Using fruit-bearing trees or trees that provide another product gives them multi-functionality.

Finally, don't forget that signage is an important responsibility of property owners. They protect you from liabilities such as someone crossing onto your land and being knocked down by one of your livestock.

Developing your property can seem like a monumental task but adding order like the processes listed above makes everything more manageable.

Checklist to follow when purchasing a homestead

Picking the right property saves you lots of costs and headaches when developing the design for your home and its surroundings. Here is a quick checklist of items that will ultimately make this process easier for you:

- Be selective if you are financing your property purchase with a bank. Choose the one that best fits your needs.
- Deal locally with smaller mortgage brokers, as this typically costs less, and the process is less of a hassle than with big banks.
- Get the full details of any type of loan that you take, such as credit terms and the size of the down payment, so that you understand just what you are getting into.
- It takes three days to close as the law allows all parties to read over the disclosure before closing.
- Be careful filing a dispute if it comes up that the asking price of the property you are interested in is higher than the appraised prices.

Sometimes the following process creates more headaches rather than solving problems.

- Know what you want before you purchase anything because if you don't, you'll ultimately be unhappy. This is likely to lead to you starting this entire process of finding the off-the-grid property that is right for you all over again.
- Make sure you have the money to back it by being able to cover closing costs and having more than you need for your down payment. Pick a good realtor who is reputable, honest, and reliable.
- Check the surroundings to know what is close to you. For example, you might find a property with a significant water source, but this is near an industrial structure that is likely to lead to contamination.

Chapter Summary

Even on a shoestring budget, you can design your off-the-grid home where you are comfortable and have all the convenience that you need. The foundation for all of this sits on a good plan and some creativity. With your budget in place, you can investigate the architectural options for your home. This is affected by factors like access to water, the typography of the land, and privacy.

With a plan in place, you can then study the home-style options that are best suited for off-gridders. These will be outlined in the next chapter.

6

THE NATURE-FRIENDLY HOMES

*a*s mentioned earlier, you are not limited to just cabin-style homes when you live off the grid. The options are wide and varied and so too, is the cost. This chapter is a simplification of what these options are and what you can expect to get for every budget.

Types of off-grid homes

Most people do not build a full-fledged house with the normal accommodations we have come to expect of modern living. In addition to the price of land, this normally costs upward of $120,000. Instead, the popular choice is to downsize. Not only does this save money, but other benefits include:

- Increased cash flow because of less expensive living space. This leads to an increased quality of life.
- Less maintenance and upkeep with less square footage.
- Less clutter and accumulation of material things.
- More time to spend on the things you love as we spend less time on cleaning and maintaining a large home.
- Less energy consumption

Structures that allow you to downsize your living space and increase your quality of life off-the-grid include:

Tiny house

A great number of off-gridders opt to build a tiny home as they are so affordable. If you are going on the small end of things, a tiny home can cost as little as $8,000. The average cost is between $30,000 and $60,000. Adding on amenities and upping the size can make the bill go higher to an extreme top of $150,000. Sticking to the average means that it does not weigh you down by paying a mortgage for decades.

Most tiny houses are no bigger than a traditional living room. Adjusting to the square footage can be a challenge, but the advantages of tiny homes are undeniable.

They force owners to take a minimalistic approach to life as there is no space to accumulate many material belongings. Their size makes them easily relocatable.

Cob house

Such homes are constructed of a mixture of plant fibers, soil, and clay. These are made into a dough-like consistency and molded into the desired layout. These homes are easy and affordable as the construction materials are sourced almost everywhere in the country. The cost of building this earth-based home varies based on how readily available the materials are, labor and size. You can learn to build this yourself. If you're worried about the stability of this structure, don't be. There are examples of cob houses standing the test of time over hundreds of years all over the globe.

Bamboo house

Bamboo houses are great for off-gridders in tropical locations as it allows good airflow. It is also great for areas that are prone to earthquakes and storms like hurricanes and typhoons. Bamboo is light and elastic and so; it absorbs shock from seismic activity and the force of high winds well compared to concrete and steel which makes buildings rigid. Typically, bamboo houses last about 10 to 50 years before the structure needs repair or replacement. But this can serve as a temporary home as you accumulate the funding to build a more permanent residence. The cost depends on how readily available bamboo is in that location, labor, and size.

Earthship house

We have mentioned these types of homes several times already. The average price of building this energy-efficient home is about $20,000. These homes allow you to lessen your carbon footprint and recycle old materials. Be aware that mold can become an issue in humid environments. If the home is not properly insulated, heating and cooling can also become issues. If you are interested in building your own Earthship house, you can hire Earthship Biotecture to do it or do it yourself.

Straw bale house

You might be wondering how a home can pass building codes if it is built with straw. But be assured that if done properly, this is more than doable. In fact, straw bale houses are a popular choice in areas that are prone to wildfires as tightly packed straw bales are three times as fire resistant to conventional walls. This type of building tends to last around 100 years. Like with bamboo and cob buildings, the price of erecting such a structure depends on your material availability, your preferences, size, and labor.

ICF cabin

ICF stands for insulating concrete forms. These are used to hold fresh concrete so that a mold forms to provide insulation for the structure being developed. ICF cabins are moisture-resistant to prevent the growth of mold. They have a lifespan of about 100 years and require little maintenance. Compared to wood cabins, these types of cabins use less energy and are more fire resistant. The cost of such a structure can be off-putting, though. The price of a 1,000-square-foot ICF cabin can range between $120,000 and $230,000.

Shipping container

This is quite the green solution to creating living quarters off the grid. No trees need to be cut down for their construction, and it allows for the reuse of any item. Containers already have the shape of a house, so they do not need to be overly adjusted to be transformed into a comfortable home. They can be moved and relocated with ease. If you want to have a bigger living space, all you must do is stack more than one container. The basic container house can be arranged for as little as $10,000.

RV and travel trailer

This is the option for people who like to move like the wind, at a minute's notice and at the whims of their heart.

They are also a great investment for vacationers. Even off-gridders who love the benefits of owning their own property like to wander on occasion. RVs and travel trailers are not tied to a permanent address. You do not have to buy land, pay property taxes, or maintain a property. All you need to do is make the upfront investment in sourcing the vehicle and have money for gas. Many states have designated parking spaces for RVs and travel trailers. Best yet, you can have all the conveniences of a typical home. You can turn this vehicle into a full home on wheels. Generally, an RV or travel trailer costs between $15,000 and $35,000. If you do not need an RV or trailer as a permanent solution for housing, one can be rented for as little as $50 per night. This all depends on the size, amenities included, and your preferences.

Some of these options are better suited for you compared to others. The climate has a lot to do with options that are still on the table. For example, a log cabin is likely not a practical choice in a tropical climate. Once the climate permits a style of off-the-grid home, it boils down to your preferences, the cost of building and maintaining that home, and how accessible essentials like medical aid, food, and water are.

Your dream house on a dream budget

Let's say you're a badass (maybe even more than you give yourself credit for) and you take a hands-on approach to building your ideal off-the-grid home. Your budget may be small, but your creativity is mighty. Costs that you will encounter building your home include:

- Design
- Materials
- Transport
- Tools and machinery
- Fittings and fixtures
- Labor
- Utilitics

You can reduce all these costs with your imagination. I am sure that you have a vision for your off-the-grid abode in your head. Put it down on paper with sketches of not only the overall structure but all its rooms. This rough template must be turned into a detailed, accurate plan that passes local building codes. You can hire out this task, but if you have the skills to do it yourself, by all means, do so.

Of course, you should pitch in and learn some of the fine arts, like masonry and carpentry, involved in constructing a home to keep labor costs low. Ideally, for safety and to make this a more enjoyable process, you should have a team. You can pay for this labor, or you can rally your friends and family to help, just like I have done with my brother in Alaska.

The first thing that needs to be done for the actual building of your home is creating the foundations. This can be made of concrete, mortar, stone, or treated wood. The exact material used to do this determines the final cost. Shop around and get the best prices and don't forget to look into recycled and reclaimed material to keep this as effective as possible. Places that can provide these items include freight companies, wholesalers, hardware stores, manufacturing facilities, salvage yards, demolition and construction sites, local dumps, and online marketplaces like Craigslist and Facebook.

Mother Nature has a host of free construction materials, like sand, stones, mud, timber, and straw, waiting to be used if you know where to look. If you have gained a plot of land with lots of trees with thick stems, look at how you can use this resource sustainably. The same can be done if this land is seated on rocky ground. You might wonder how conservative such a practice is. And to be honest, it is not if you do not follow up with replacing this resource that you have used up.

For example, you can plant three trees for everyone that you cut down.

If your land does not provide the resources you need, investigate what is popular and readily available close by as these will be the cheapest options. This will also decrease transportation costs. If possible, get your own truck to do this. If not, shop around for a rental and negotiate with suppliers for the lowest delivery costs to keep transportation costs as low as possible.

Use the right tools and equipment to harness these resources during the build process. It saves you time and money at the end of the day. Taking shortcuts usually means higher costs in the long run. For example, you might use an ax to cut down the trees to be used to build a cabin, but a sawmill is a more practical solution that gets the job done faster, easier, and more accurately, even though it is more costly upfront. It will pay for itself as time passes. When it is done, it's time for you to sell it if you like. Don't forget that this does not have to be brand new. You can buy second-hand tools and equipment.

If you are using timber, be mindful of using harmful chemicals to treat the wood. This is ultimately not good for your health or the environment. Anything with long, drawn-out explanations or graphics with cross-bones and skulls should be avoided. There are eco-friendly options for treating wood like Linseed Oil and Pine Tar.

Other tools (power and hand) that you are likely to need include:

- Excavators
- Front-end loaders
- Concrete mixers
- Generator lighting and powering tools
- Auger
- Saws such as circular, miter, and reciprocating
- Nailers
- Table Saw
- Drill
- Impact Driver
- Magnetic Bit Storage Bit Holder
- Oscillating Multi Tool
- Planer
- Jigsaw
- Angle Grinder
- Hammers
- Pliers
- Wrench
- Chisel

- Screwdrivers
- Axes
- Knives
- Tape measures
- Speed Square
- String Lines
- Chalk Lines
- Levels

All these tools and equipment might not be relevant to your project, so use your discretion when picking from this list.

When it comes to utilities, keep your cost down by using what is the most available in that location. For example, if you have a fast-flowing river or lake on your property, it is wise to install a mini hydroelectric station. On the other hand, if your location is windy, install a wind turbine. Solar power is only practical in consistently sunny locations, so if your area sees half the year without sunlight, this type of energy might not be the best for you. Be sure to also have a backup source of power like firewood, kerosene, diesel, or propane. They might not be the best for your conservation efforts (hence why they aren't your preferred source of energy) but they will do in a pinch. They are also reliable, cheap, have a relatively long shelf life and store well.

Building your own home can be an intimidating task no matter how you do it. But as an off-gridder, I know

you've got just the right stuff in you to see this through. You can do this. It's easier than you think. But that realization will only sink in when you get started and get into the thick of things.

Inspiring designs for your off-grid home

To help spark the creative juices in your noggin, here is a list of off-the-grid home designs in remote locations and with environmental consciousness in mind. Feel free to look up the designs of these homes to see which inspires you.

- The Hut in Ohio, USA, designed by Midland Architecture
- The House of the Big Arch in South Africa is almost a 2 hours drive to the nearest town.
- The 124-square-foot tiny home called The Athru
- Catuçaba, powered by wind turbines and solar panels in Brazil
- The Edifice created by Marc Thorpe with its rooftop solar panels and lighting facilitated by candles

- The tiny cabin, Ashen Cabin with no power or running water for a lifestyle far removed from modern living
- Heva, the timber cabin that is a 22-square meter tiny home in France.

Chapter Summary

There are many home-style options for off-the-grid living spaces. These options include tiny homes, cob homes, Earthship houses, and RVs. Which of these you choose depends on the climate, your preferences, the cost, and the availability of essentials like water and food. You can create a home that fits your style and preference even on a budget with a creative mind and an eye for looking for bargains, using natural resources, and recycling old materials.

So far, we have looked at off-the-grid home designs above ground but what about the options below that surface? Let's look at that next.

7

OFF-GRIDING 6-FEET UNDER

*T*he cold war lasted a very long time, and people had to find creative ways of protecting themselves and their families. Personalized underground bunkers gained popularity in one such way. With the threat of nuclear war around the corner, it made sense to seek cover underground to avoid the radiation. Fortunately, this nuclear implosion did not come to pass, but the benefits of an underground home cannot be denied. These benefits are becoming more apparent, especially with the troubles experienced during the covid-19 pandemic. This chapter looks at what these benefits are and what options best suit off-gridders.

Underground homes as an off-the-grid option

To understand the advantages of an underground home, you first need to grasp the concept of what it is. So, let's start by defining this type of shelter. Underground homes are dwellings built beneath the ground's surface. Even though I mentioned the rise in popularity of underground structures during the Cold War, this type of home has been part of many cultures for thousands of years. From the freezing conditions of the Arctic and Iceland to the scorching deserts of Australia, homes that are partially or entirely buried underground have been used because of the unique exploits that come with their creation.

Such homes are energy efficient because they are less susceptible to extreme temperatures, whether hot or cold, that affect the surface. The indoor temperature is easier to maintain, and wild fluctuations with changing temperatures can be avoided. This makes for a comfortable home that requires little artificial cooling or heating. The temperatures of many such homes are maintained with passive solar heating. This system captures sunlight in the material that this structure is made of and then releases that heat when the sunlight is absent, like at night.

Besides the protection against extreme weather and energy savings, privacy is another advantage of building this type of home. You don't have to worry about your neighbors peeking over the fence with this home.

There are potential downsides to building such a home, and that includes the cost of excavating and water-proofing this abode. These activities add about 25% to the existing building cost of a home. However, the cost is normally offset by the savings gained in yearly energy usage. If the home is not well built, then humidity and ventilation issues will arise. But the keywords here are "not well built". A properly constructed underground home will not have such issues. Condensation can be prevented by incorpo-rating more insulation into the home's designs. Include a ventilator to ensure the exchange of indoor and outdoor air to remove air quality concerns.

Root cellars

Before we move on to actual types of underground homes, let's look at an underground feature that you can consider adding to your home even if it is 6 feet over. That feature is called a root cellar. A root cellar is an underground structure used to store food. Tradi-tionally, this space was used to store fruits, veggies, and other types of produce. However, with a few modifica-tions, you can store and even extend the shelf life of other foods, including meats and dairy products.

Food storage should not be an afterthought, especially hard-to-source items like fruits and veggies that provide essential nutrients like vitamins and minerals. It needs to be at the forefront of your mind. The average American has less than three days' worth of food stored in case of emergencies. As we saw with grocery shelves being wiped out within minutes and many people being left without the food items needed to survive during the covid-19 pandemic, everyone needs to have a stockpile of food for emergencies. Off-gridders need to double down on this activity as it is quite normal for residents to be further away from modern conveniences like supermarkets. You need to have at least two weeks' worth of food stored. Ideally, though, this stock should last you at least 6 months, but you can build up to this amount.

Where and how you store this food determines its shelf life. It's no use having all this food if it spoils quickly. Root cellars can be kept at the optimal temperature and other necessary conditions, like appropriate lighting and humidity to keep food from spoiling prematurely. This saves you time and money and gives you peace of mind, knowing that you are prepared for dire times.

There are different types of root cellars. First, the basement root cellar allows for easy attachment to the main living unit. All you must do is use the foundation walls of your home to set this up. Create walls in the basement with studs and boards. Keep the heat out by insulating the ceilings, walls, and doors. This must be done with any ducts or pipes in the space, too. A ventilation system must also be added to remove stale air and bring in fresh air. This prevents the growth of mildew and mold.

The next type of root cellar is called a hole-in-the-ground cellar. This is not connected to the house like the first option. Instead, it is a horizontal hole dug into the ground. The conditions for developing this food storage unit are:

- Soil with good drainage like sand.
- A hole dug deep enough to maintain an appropriate temperature of 32º to 40ºF (0° to 4.5°C). This depth should be at least 10 feet.
- Flaring the sides of the hole to prevent cave-ins.

The hole should also be lined with brown material like dried leaves and straw. When construction is done, build a thick wooden lid to cover the hole and cover the lid with soil.

If you're low on space or facing an emergency, a garbage can may serve as a makeshift root cellar. This is particularly useful in winter. Dig a hole that allows the can to sit 4" below the soil's level and is just slighter wider than the can's diameter. Add brown material inside the can along with the stored food. Cover the lid with this material along with plastic to keep everything nice and dry.

How to build an underground home

Unfortunately (or fortunately, depending on how you look at it), you cannot just get to digging to construct an underground home. There is a right and a wrong way to go about it. The right way includes an initial step of developing a blueprint suitable for an underground home. Luxury is not the typical first thought with this type of home even though, by no means, do you have to live down in the dumps. However, underground homes are mainly built for security and safety. These homes normally feature combined spaces that equal an open floor plan, wall-mounted furniture to save space, and the use of vertical space for storage. Claustrophobia can be a cause for concern with the efficiency used to construct these homes so plan this design with 5 to 10 square feet of space allocated to everyone that will live there.

Permission is needed to build this humble abode. These permissions, in addition to the approval of the house plan, include:

- Grading permits for altering the typography of the land with excavations and fillings
- Building permits for adhering to construction laws
- Discretionary permits to affect the surrounding area as little as possible
- Plumbing permits
- Electrical permits

The location where this house is built also matters, just like with a conventional above-the-ground dwelling. This place needs to be safe for all. Avoid places that are:

- Near large bodies of water to prevent flooding
- Near flammable materials
- Surrounded by lots of trees and other flora. Digging up near these means dealing with root systems that can affect the ecosystem in those areas and raise costs
- Near utility lines

If any of these features become a concern, re-evaluate where you will place your underground home.

Building starts with choosing the right material so that your home does not fold underneath the weight of dirt. Wood is a poor choice as it weathers, is not waterproof, and is susceptible to rot and infestation. It can be used to decorate the inside of this type of home, though. Popular materials for building an underground home include:

- Metal sheeting. This can be quite expensive, and costs only go up because insulation needs to be added, but it is water-resistant and holds up well. Because of this, shipping contains make great underground homes. They would need to be reinforced though, as they were not built for that purpose and their layout is not very customizable.
- Concrete. The self-healing variety can last up to 200 years with little maintenance. This is also sturdy and cheaper than metal sheeting.
- Bricks. They are also sturdy and affordable. They are quite weatherproof and make great insulators. Also, they add a little panache to what could seem like an otherwise drab design.

This leads to a discussion on integrating materials that will make life comfortable. You do not want to invest all this time, energy, and money into a home that will make you feel like being somewhere else. As a result, here is a list of must-have items that will make your underground home cool, comfy, and hygienic:

- A ventilator to price clean air. NBC filters are great for emergencies
- Water filters to ensure a supply of clean water
- UV filters are an option.
- A generator to provide power
- A waste removal system with a pump and lift to ensure waste does not accumulate.

With those considerations in place, you can then start digging! This starts with choosing the right excavation equipment. A fork and shovel are definite no-nos. You need digging instruments that allow accuracy, efficiency, and quickness and can fit in tight and awkward spaces. Trenchers and excavators are the right choices.

Digging must be done with safety in mind. A systematic approach looks like this:

1. Digging a trench. Start by cutting the trench wall at an angle to build steps that allow traveling up the wall. This process is called sloping or benching-creating. Next, create a support system that prevents the removed dirt from falling. Finally, create a trench shield to protect the people inside the trench.
2. Creating a support system. Reinforced or self-healing concrete is the best. Materials for setting the foundation as they don't crack

easily. Placing metal beams across the trench prevents the home from collapsing in on itself. Using reinforced concrete gives an added layer of protection.

3. Placing the living structure. Ensure that the walls are 1 to 3 feet thick. Coat these with water-proofing material like rubberized asphalt. If this home is in an area prone to earthquakes, use earthquake-proofing devices like cross braces and shear walls.

4. Covering the home. Do not cover the home with over 10 feet of packed dirt.

Chapter Summary

Underground homes offer a variety of benefits to off-gridders, including protection against extreme weather, energy savings, and privacy. The potential downsides like the increased cost associated with excavation and fillings, ventilation, and condensation, can be mitigated with proper planning and practice during construction.

To build an off-the-grid underground home you need to:

- Develop a design focused on security, safety, and the efficient use of space.

- Getting the permissions needed before starting construction.
- Using the right materials like brick for building this home.
- Installing materials that make life comfortable like ventilators and water filtration.
- Dig the ground using the right equipment such as a trencher and excavator.

We have looked at homes that are 6 feet under. The next chapter dives into the details of a home on wheels.

8

_____

THE HOUSE THAT MOVES

e have been conditioned into thinking that a permanent foundation is the only right way to set up a home that you are comfortable in and proud of. But we have challenged the norms with off-grid living. So, why should we not challenge what a "home" means? A home is not about where or how you set the foundation. A home is where your heart is at peace. Some people find that peace in the stability offered by laying cast in an abode that has pillars speared into the ground. Other people's hearts yearn for continuous adventure and fresh sights. No rule says their home cannot go where they go. You may be convinced (or even intrigued) by the idea of living off-grid. And living in a mobile house on top of it may seem a surreal way of living, which it is!

But do not rule it out as something that can become your everyday life. This chapter explores what it means to have a home on wheels and how you can get your own if that is the right choice for you.

To make this determination, let's answer a few frequently asked questions about having a trailer home:

How practical is it to live in a mobile home?

You can make living in a mobile home a feasible option by incorporating all the elements you need to make living a comfortable and safe home.

Will you be able to adjust to such a lifestyle?

There might be an adjustment period, but as you become accustomed to the nuances of living in such a home, you might find such a home resonates with you more than a home with a permanent foundation.

What are the legalities of owning a mobile home?

Most mobile homes are not subject to the regulations of building codes in most states because they are not considered a structure. This is a double-edged sword. The legalities of designing and building a mobile home are more relaxed compared to those of a house with a permanent foundation, but you want to be safe and sound in your home when all is said and done. Take the necessary building codes into consideration as you consider the structure of your mobile home.

What are the zoning requirements?

A mobile home might legally be considered an RV in many states depending on the size. As such you can park your mobile home in camping locations. To do this, however, you may have to register your mobile home with the Recreation Vehicle Industry Association (RVIA) and comply with building according to their standards.

Do you need any permits to own or travel with a mobile home?

You do need to be permitted to travel with a travel trailer used residential and above certain square footage recognized by the state.

IT IS best to seek the advice of local mobile home experts to get all the logistics and obligations sorted out before you create your mobile home. Once you have the legalities of owning a mobile home out of the way, you can move on to enjoying the benefits.

Building your trailer home

Although exciting, building a mobile home from scratch is a challenging task...That you are more than capable of accomplishing with some creativity and fortitude. Remember, what you can achieve as an off-gridder is only limited by your mindset. With the right perception, anything is possible. Creating a mobile home is possible as long as you plan well and do your math right.

There are three approaches that you can take when creating the mobile home of your dreams. First, you can build from a kit. Such kits provide pre-formed or pre-cut pieces, and you put the parts together yourself. The accuracy of these fittings allows the homeowner to save on energy costs as they are supposed to fit snuggly and discourage draughts that can decrease energy efficiency. Such homes are designed so that people with no experience can do the assembly. On the upside, such a home comes up quickly. You can be assured that the home is structurally sound as its design meets building codes.

The possible downsides of using kits include receiving damaged material from the manufacturer and limited flexibility in the home design. You also miss the experience of building your own home.

That possible disadvantage leads to the next approach that you can take in creating a mobile home, which is building it from scratch. Taking on the process allows you to have a final product that is exactly what you want. You can rack in the savings from labor costs as you are doing this yourself.

The first process involved in DIYing a mobile home is designing the mobile home. The design must have the following characteristics:

- Align with your budget
- Function so that you have everything you need in a living space
- Be structurally sound and pass building codes.
- Understand how utilities will be incorporated into the layout of your home.
- Match the towing vehicle of your choice

The trailer frame affects how mobile your trailer home is. The trailer must support the weight of the final build. You can also DIY the frame, but this is very challenging, and one slight mistake can be costly. It is easy to source an older trailer no longer in use and use the chassis.

Once the trailer frame is secured, you build the shell of the home onto it, so you don't have the hassle of doing that move later. Proper support must be built with a structure that will later be developed with the addition of walls, roof, and floor. Construction options for the shell are wood or metals like steel and aluminum.

As you build this mobile home, be precise. Mistakes can cost you comfort and peace of mind in the long run. Outsource projects that need an expert touch like electrical installations. Building your own mobile home is a time-intensive task but highly rewarding at the end of the day.

Finally, you can find a middle ground between building kits and creating from scratch by using a pre-built shell. The use of shipping containers as shells is a current trend. From there, you can customize and DIY the rest.

Chapter Summary

Some people love the stability offered by an abode with a permanent foundation. Other people's hearts yearn for continuous adventure and new sights. A mobile home is the perfect fit for that latter set of people and can even offer the former set of people a means of vacationing unconventionally.

You can take any of the three following options to create the mobile home:

1. Build from a kit
2. Build from scratch
3. Use a pre-built shell.

We have opened your mind to the possibilities that exist with different types of homes, including a home that moves. The next chapter dives into how you can ensure this home is stocked with food that always meets your nutritional needs.

9

WINNING YOUR DAILY BREAD

*H*unger pains are not enjoyable in the least. Many people have the misconception that off-gridders are always on the verge of starvation. But that is far from the truth... if they are prepared, that is. Let's ensure that you're prepared to provide food for yourself and your family, no matter where you choose to live. Not only that, but this chapter will also teach you how to find nutrition in times of emergency and how you can stock up on food you enjoy munching on rather than just the essentials.

Foraging tips

Foraging is the act of gathering food in the wild. This can be both plant products and animal products.

Therefore, picking an apple as you stalk through the woods and eating it is considered foraging. So is eating dandelions, edible weeds that grow in your garden. If a plant or animal grows without human interference and is consumed, it is considered foraging.

Foraging is not just something that is done for survival. It can be taken up as a hobby, too. I love to forage to get in some exercise while I explore and learn more about that environment. It is truly a way to connect with Mother Nature and appreciate the seeds she sows. The food is free, and you get to try new flavors and perhaps supplement your diet with more nutrition. It can also be a sustainable practice. Let's say you picked that apple. When you're done, simply throw the core with the seeds back into the environment, and as easy as that, you have planted the next generation of apple trees.

In addition to providing food, foraged items can be used medicinally. The kicker is that you cannot just go about picking plants or hunting animals without knowledge of what these parts will do for you or to you and how you can use them safely. Educate yourself about the local flora and fauna that can be foraged in your location.

A few tips to help you start a safe foraging journey include:

- Accessing reading material, perhaps from local libraries or online, about the edible and medicinal plants that exist in that region. You can also talk to locals to find out the plants that are foraged. You must learn to spot the features of these plants to avoid poisoning.
- Unfortunately, many safe-to-consume and poisonous plants have some of the same features as similar leaf structures or flowers that look alike. You must know the similarities and the differences to tell them apart.
- Refrain from eating anything brightly colored or red while foraging as many poisonous plants produce vibrantly colored plant parts like flowers and fruits. Only eat or use a plant part after you have positively identified it.
- Do a quick test for edibility by rubbing the plant on your wrist or touching it with your tongue. If you experience an allergic reaction like a rash or a burning sensation, discard the plant and seek medical assistance.
- Get comfortable with mollusks and worms as you will be digging up roots if you take up foraging seriously. They can also be found along the length of plants, especially if their plants are creepers and crawlers. The same can be said about the presence of insects. This is a

sign that the plants are healthy to consume as other creatures are feasting.

Despite how fun it can be, foraging can be a challenging activity. It requires the practitioner to have patience, determination, and most importantly, the skills to locate, catch or hunt food. Particularly with foraging for animals, there are a few skills that are useful to have under your belt. Making rope is one of them. A rope has a variety of uses in the wild. Making and securing shelter. Creating a clothesline. To make a splint to apply pressure to a wound. All of these and more are uses of rope outside of its use in food-sourcing and food-keeping activities. To make a basic length of rope, break the branches and top off a plant with lots of fiber. Clean and tenderize these fibers. Do this by wetting and rubbing them between your thumbs. They will soften and separate. Allow them to dry and then twist together to form bends and kinks.

More useful skills to learn as a forager include making primitive weapons. They can be used to hunt and to maintain personal safety. Primitive weapons that can be fashioned in the wild include stone ax heads, a bow and arrow, and spears. Another skill that makes you a more competent hunter includes learning to set traps for small game. Such traps include ground snares, spring traps, and deadfall traps. Before you can trap those animals though, you need to learn to track them. That takes powers of stealth. Trapping bigger game also requires those skills but practice with small game before you graduate to hunting larger ones.

I also suggest getting better at fishing. A fishing line and hook are the best options for this activity, but if you are in the wild, spearfishing works just as well. All you must do is wade into the water or find a good spot on the water's edges. Patience is the name of the game from there. Once you spot a fish, shove the spear into the water and try to impale the fish. It takes practice to get this right, but you've got this!

How to source food in the wild

Many off-gridders want to get as far removed from modern life as we know it as possible. Therefore, they are situated away from your usual grocery store. In some cases, Amazon cannot deliver to that remote zip code. No woe-is-me music is needed though because if that is the off-grid lifestyle that you have chosen, you simply need to gain alternate sources for taking care of your daily bread. There are several food systems that you can practice for sourcing food. Gardening is one such option. Many types of gardening can be pursued, including container gardening, raised-bed gardening, window box gardening, and more. You can combine these methodologies to get the most variety of crops.

Add a bit of sophistication to your gardening operation by learning to perform the following farming activities:

Testing the soil's type

Different soils are better for the growth of different types of plants. For example, vegetables grow better in sandy, loamy soil. Determining this allows you to develop a list of crops that will be best suited for the conditions of that location.

Practicing no-till gardening

No-till gardening is the practice of letting organic matter like dried leaves decompose to become the topsoil on the ground. You must not disturb this layer as you plant into it. This allows microbes and creatures such as worms to do the best work in aiding your plants to grow. By allowing this organic matter to decompose in this way, you are essentially composting.

Set up an irrigation system

Your irrigation system can be as simple as a hose. However, spending all day watering plants is not ideal. An irrigation system does not have to be complicated, though. If you have a nearby water source, use the force of gravity to route that water to your garden. Alternatively, you can use an industrial setup with drip tape and overhead irrigation.

Plan your crop selection

After understanding the growing conditions of the location and with irrigation and no-till gardening setup, it's time to plan what you will grow in your garden. Research what grows best in the area. Develop a list of viable options from this. From that list, decide what you like to eat. It makes no sense to start this journey of growing crops that you do not enjoy eating. This will only discourage you from the practice. After you have gotten a hang of the process, then you can start incorporating more adventurous crops into your lists. Remember that it is an option to sell, barter or give away the excess items that your taste buds do not agree with. Save the seeds from your harvest to save on buying seeds. Wash and dry these seeds. Place different seeds in individual jars, and label and date these. You can also freeze your seeds if you plan to sow them at a later date.

Storing harvests

It's no good if you put all that time and effort into gardening only to have your crops wasted because you couldn't eat through them fast enough. Save yourself that heartache by learning preservation methods like canning, fermenting, drying, and freezing. Preserving your foods also allows you to enjoy your favorites outside the seasons they usually grow.

Remember to label and place the date they were made on the preserved products. Food poisoning will be your reality if you consume them inappropriately, and that is no fun.

You need to have a place to store these foods and their preserved counterparts in your home. You do not have to rely on a root cellar alone. A wine cellar works, and so does an adequately sized pantry.

Gardening can take up quite a bit of time, even with a small size. Anticipate this and schedule the time so that you do not get flustered. Plan planting times based on the proper seasons for different plants. You also need to schedule harvesting and food preservation. The effort you place into this will be worth the reward.

Raising animals is an excellent option for adding protein to your diet. Popularly reared animals include cows, goats, rabbits, chickens, and fish. You might be tempted to get all these animals and others as soon as you start your livestock-raising adventure, but if you're new to this practice, start small with one or two animals and slowly increase your fold as you gain footing. Look into which animals are commonly reared in the area and network with people raising them to get tips and advice. You can even work together with these people to develop a barter system so that you don't have to raise all these animals to get variety. You can raise what they don't have, and you can exchange.

Livestock requires good nutrition to grow big, strong, and healthy, just like humans. The easiest way to have a fresh supply of feed is to grow it yourself. You can grow everyday items like wheat, rye, and oats during the winter. Extra veggies and fruits can feed pigs and chickens. Goats and sheep love grass and can eat free-range. Most animals will eat table scraps, so you can save them and distribute them safely.

If you're feeling exotic, you can try your hand at insect farming. Insects are raised and bred like livestock. They are called microstock or mini livestock in that case.

As mentioned earlier, you can gain two types of food, crops and fish, through aquaponics. Another water-based activity for growing plants is called hydroponics. Hydroponics allows the growing of plants without soil. Instead, plants are fed mineral salts dissolved in water.

Don't keep all your eggs in one basket when sourcing food. There is no one perfect off-grid food supply system. Learn multiple ways of sourcing food in case one fails. It is best to have at least 5.

Chapter Summary

Providing food for yourself and your family off-the-grid does not have to be a headache. All it takes is planning and foresight. Gardening is a common way of making this provision. Grow the best crops with activities like testing soil and the installation of irrigation. Foraging and hunting are also viable ways of supplying your daily bread in addition to others like aquaponics.

Next, let's look at how to keep hydrated off-the-grid and outdoors.

10

STAYING HYDRATED IN THE OUTDOORS

$\mathcal{T}$his chapter is all about water. Composed of 2 hydrogen atoms and 1 oxygen atom, it has the simple chemical formula $H2O$. Each molecule of water has a few staying properties. In its purest state, it is:

- Transparent
- Tasteless
- Odorless
- Inorganic (meaning it can't be derived from any other living matter)

Water takes up 70% of this planet's surface. From afar, the water in our oceans and seas looks blue, hence why the earth has been dubbed with the fond title the "big, blue planet."

What is the most essential feature of water? H2O is needed to keep us alive. Water is found abundantly in our universe... in its gaseous form. Evidence supports there may be water in liquid form under the surface of some planets and other celestial bodies. But is it only earth that has liquid water populating its surface - from polar ice caps to jutting geysers and even in and around volcanoes and deserts - and so supports the formation and continuation of life. Where there is water, there is life.

All our bodily systems and functions depend on it to keep on working. The flowing liquid state of water allows easy transfer from cell to cell within bodies like our own. And so, because of water, we can breathe, digest food, have the energy to do anything, think, feel, and even produce waste.

But water is not just essential for maintaining a healthy, balanced body. It is also vital for keeping our external environment clean and healthy. You need water to cook, do laundry, for sanitation, and more. It is only because of water we can sustain our livelihoods, ensure school attendance, build upstanding communities, and do all the other activities we attribute to daily life.

Without water, life on or off-the-grid would be impossible.

We have mentioned the importance of locating and supplying water to your off-the-grid home several times in this book, but it really needs the spotlight shined on it without interruption. Therefore, this chapter is dedicated to showing you:

- How to locate safe drinking and usable water.
- How to supply your off-grid home with this water once you have found it.

Identifying signs of water nearby

It might be a little worse to wear, but the human body can go for three weeks without food. Depending on the situation, months can go by without proper consumption of food. The body needs the energy it derives from food to do even the smallest tasks like blinking or sighing. When food is eaten in plentiful amounts, the body has all the energy it needs to keep on producing the fuel it requires. When food is in short supply, the body enters a state of starvation and functions differently so that it does not burn as much energy.

There is a stipulation for this to be a reality. This person must drink water. The situation becomes much direr without water. A human being cannot survive over three days without the liquid. That number goes down quickly if the climate is harsh or other factors are at play, like suffering from health conditions. Even going just 24 hours without water severely depletes mental and physical strength, which makes it difficult to perform the tasks necessary to keep alive. These effects are caused by a state called dehydration. It occurs when the body uses and loses more water than it intakes. Extreme thirst notwithstanding, other effects of dehydration include (but are not limited to):

- Headaches
- Dizziness
- Decreased skin elasticity
- Low blood pressure
- Dry mouth

That is only the beginning, though. Severe dehydration leads to seizures, kidney failure, swelling in the brain, shock, and coma. These are steps leading to death.

With those facts in mind, I don't think I need to stress how important it is to know how to fetch clean and safe drinking water. It is a matter of survival. Any old amount will not do! The human body needs between 2 and 3 liters of water every day for optimum functioning. If you're sick, in extremely cold or hot temperatures, or exerted, then the amount goes up.

The history of human life is not one where we had water flowing through our taps until recently on the timescale. We had to work hard to get our thirst quenched and our bodies clean. In modern times, most of us have become accustomed to the conveniences of the utility provided by water companies. But what if you get unceremoniously removed from this convenience? It can seem like a far-fetched situation, but the news is filled with stories of people who become lost in the wilderness with no shelter, no food, and no water for days, sometimes weeks, and even months on end. Their miraculous survival was only possible because they found and used a source of water through more than likely unconventional means.

Knowing how to locate water is not just an important skill to know if you get lost or are stranded. It is also a must for off-gridders who are likely not tied to the main water utility. It wastes time and energy to just go off on a tangent looking, so it is a must that you develop an awareness of the signs that water may be nearby.

These clues include:

The presence of green foliage

Plants also need water to survive as humans do, so their presence shows that water is in that environment. This is a particularly useful hint in deserts or arid conditions. A group of plants in that area indicates that a creek or other water body may be in the vicinity. It is best to get to a higher elevation to scope out the area to spot foliage like this.

The presence of wildlife

Animals need water to live as well. They tend to move toward water bodies, so if you see a group of birds circling nearby or paw tracks, follow where they lead. You just might be surprised to find a watering hole. Different types of birds are indicative of different sources of water. Finches are water drinkers and eat grain. During dry spells, colonies of finches congregate near water, typically in the form of a hidden spring. You can apply the same analogy to other types of grain-eating birds like sparrows, mourning doves, redpolls, and goldfinches. A few exceptions to this rule are cockatoos and parrots. They are not reliable indicators of nearby water sources.

Flesh-eating birds like eagles, owls, hawks, and falcons are not reliable indicators of nearby sources of water either. They get the moisture they need from the blood of their prey.

Seed-eating birds like wild pigeons spend daytime hours in feeding plains but look for water when dusk approaches. They have their fill of water and return to the nesting grounds. The way these birds fly can indicate the direction in which water can be found. If they are flying slowly and moving from tree to tree, the birds have likely come from drinking water. On the other hand, if they're moving swiftly and low, they're flying toward the water. The best time to follow them to find water is during these periods of low swift flight.

Mammals need to drink water regularly to stay alive. This applies even to the carnivores of the bunch. However, some animals can travel quite a long distance from water sources and go for long periods between drinks. Some animals never travel far from water, and you can rely on their presence to hint at water availability. Wild pigs, for example. A good rule of thumb for using animals to find water is to look for regular animal trails.

Reptiles tend not to be good indicators of water because they are hydrated by blood from prey and dew in the environment.

The presence of insects

This is a particularly useful hint if you live in a place with a high mosquito population. These insects need water to breed and so stay close to these sources. Bees also build their hives between three and five miles of water.

Ants stay close to water as well and tend to create their nest near one. If you see a trail of black ants climbing a tree and disappearing into a hole, there is likely a hidden pool of water within the trunk. To find out if this is true, dip a long stick into the hole. If it comes out wet, you've struck not gold but water. Do not chop down the tree to get to the water though. You don't want to destroy the ecosystem in that tree or stop it from being a supply of water in the future. Instead, make the hole bigger using a knife if it is small. Use a rag or create a mop by tying grasses together. Dip either into the water and squeeze the liquid into a collection device. Alternatively, you can use a straw or long, hollow device to suck the water up before dumping it into your collection device.

Another insect that is a certain signal of nearby water is the Mason fly. Their buildings are created a few hundred yards from water - wet soil, to be more exact. The flies hover, drop to such spots, and create pallets of mud. Investigate this behavior, and you just might find a spring.

Low-lying terrain

Rainwater tends to collect on flat land. The same is true for runoff from mountainous or hilly regions as water moves from higher elevations to lower ones. Examples of such terrain include depressions, crevices, and valleys.

Damp sand or dirt

This dampness indicates the presence of water. This can come from rainfall or being saturated by a nearby water body.

Water-containing flora

Cacti is a classic example of this type of plant. Cacti is a type of succulent. The structure of succulents is designed to store water in the stems and roots so that the plant survives long periods without water. If a succulent appears healthy and is fully hydrated, this is a sign that water may be nearby.

Succulents may also serve as a source of water. In fact, finding the right succulent can relieve thirst in an emergency. All you must do is break a 3-feet length of the branch or roots. Stand the piece in a trough made of bark and allow the liquid to drain into a collection device. The amount of water can be so great that it gushes from the plant when it is cut.

Be mindful of a few points as you cannot indiscriminately drink from succulents and other plants containing liquids. For those found to be a healthy source of water, do not keep the cut piece for more than 24 hours as the part starts to go bad after then. The liquid changes and can become dangerous to consume. Any plant with a milky or colored sap should be strictly avoided. Not only is the sap likely to be poisonous if consumed but it can also cause skin irritation.

Just looking at the plant is not a good judge of the drinkability of the liquids within its parts. Only the positive ID of the plant serves as a good judge. Here are a few examples of plants whose liquid may be safe to drink. The branches and roots of eucalyptus (also called gum trees) can be safe to drink. However, the leaves of the plant contain oil that is poisonous to human beings. In tropical areas, vines like monkey ropes and lianas can provide safe drinking water.

Even if you have positively identified a plant as safe to drink from, do a taste test before drinking the water. Even if the water is transparent, taste a small amount of the liquid. If it is completely or almost tasteless, it is likely safe to drink.

Common sources of water in the outdoors

Some of the most popular water bodies you may spot follow the signs listed below. I will include a brief note on these as well as how you can safely collect water from them. Before we get to this list, I must explicitly state that when you find these sources of water, the water must not be directly consumed. It must be first filtered and then purified before you drink the liquid. This is the only way to remove any possible harmful bacteria. Water is life. However, water can lead to your death if it contains pathogens.

On this planet, almost 1 billion people do not have access to a reliable clean supply of water and so water-borne diseases are rampant. Diarrhea is a common sign of contracting a waterborne disease, and over 2 million deaths are recorded every year because unsafe water was used for hygiene and consumption and led to diarrheal disease.

Waterborne illnesses are sicknesses caused by drinking or recreationally using water that is contaminated with microbes that cause disease. These are scary little buggers, but they do not easily reveal themselves. Most people would abstain from drinking water that no longer carries the properties of pure water. They would stay away from water that is cloudy-looking or muddy. They would stay away from water that emits a foul odor. They would spit out the water that tastes suspicious. But sometimes, contaminated water looks and tastes as you would expect pure water. You cannot rely on your eyes or taste buds as an accurate test for harmful pathogens. There are rapid test kits that allow for identifying the presence of some waterborne pathogens, but the safest action you can take is to filter the water to remove microbes large enough to be captured by the sieve and then purify to kill any that remain.

Five common ways of filtering and purifying water include:

Boiling

This simple method kills bacteria that cannot withstand temperatures above 212°F (100°C). The water must be at a rolling boil for at least 2 minutes before it is deemed safe. This time is increased to 3 minutes at elevations above 6,500 feet.

Distillation

This process involves heating water so that it evaporates. They collected the water that had condensed after evaporation, which was free of contaminants, to be safely consumed.

Solar purification

With this approach, sunlight may shine through the water. The water is placed in a clear container, such as a plastic bottle, and then positioned horizontally to catch the maximum sunlight. The UV rays damage the structure of the microbes and prevent them from reproducing. The process takes several hours to complete. Adding lime juice decreases this time but also changes the taste of the water.

An electric water purifier

This electronic device purifies water with multiple stages that involve both UV and UF filtration and modern water filtration technology.

Disinfection tablets

Such tablets contain compounds like iodine and chlorine dioxide that kill pathogens. Each type of tablet comes with a unique set of instructions. Follow the directions on the package to purify the water. Usually, the water is left to sit for a directed amount of time so the tablets can be effective.

There are many other ways to filter and purify water, but those listed above are a good start. Now that we have had a brief discussion about making water safe to drink, let's get to sources.

Streams, rivers, and lakes

These are the typical imagery we develop when we hear water bodies, but we cannot just go diving and dipping into these without thought. Flowing water is the safest option as this action makes it harder for bacteria to accumulate. Therefore, streams and rivers are usually a safer bet in that circumstance. Lakes and ponds are normally still as they don't drain away. It is easier for microorganisms to grow in such an environment. While this is not absolutely the case every time, it is better to stay on the side of caution if you have the option.

Smaller water bodies like streams are preferred over larger ones because larger ones are more likely to be polluted upstream.

Collecting water from the sources can be as simple as using a container to dip into them, such as during emergencies or during activities such as camping and hiking, or more complicated, such as running piping systems from the source to another area.

Rainwater

Rainwater in rural environments is the safer bet, as rainwater in urban environments can travel through pollution, such as vehicle emissions. If you are caught out in the wild, collect rainwater in containers. Ultimately, you may tie the corners of a tarp or similar object around trees nearby. Allow this to hang a few feet off the ground and create a depression in the center with a small rock. You may then collect the water that has accumulated there.

Morning dew

All you must do to collect this type of water is walk through tall grass or in a meadow with absorbent clothes before sunrise. When the cloth becomes saturated, wring out the water and repeat. Alternatively, tufts of fine grass can be used in the same way.

Plant transpiration

Think of transpiration like the plant sweating. Moisture escapes as vapor in the atmosphere around the plant, particularly from its leaves. Collect this water first thing in the morning before the sunshine dries it away. Tie a plastic around the leafy part of the plant. Weigh the bag down so that the water collects at the bottom by using a rock. The leaves will continue to transpire throughout the day, and the bag will collect this moisture. Never collect water from a poisonous plant.

Fruits and vegetation

Succulents, fruits, vegetables, and even roots contain a lot of water. These sources of water are particularly useful in tropical environments where they are abundant. For example, coconut, a tropical fruit, contains water in the center. Break open the hard outer shell to access this.

Tree crotches and rock crevices

The amount of water collected from such places is not a lot but, in an emergency, anything is better than nothing. To remove water from these areas, stick a clean piece of cloth into the crack or hole. Allow it to soak up the water and then wring it out. Repeat this if possible. Water is easier to find in such locations after the rain has fallen.

Underground still

This is a human-manufactured source of water. This works by allowing the collection of condensation that works due to heat from the sun striking the ground.

Supplies needed to create this are a container (as large as you have), clear plastic sheeting, a tool for digging, rocks, and a tube like a straw or a piece of bamboo. To create this water source:

1. Dig a pit that is 3 feet wide and 3 feet deep in an area that receives sunlight for most of the day.
2. Insert the container into the pit and run the tube out of the hole.

3. Place the sheeting over the hole and use soil and rocks to keep it in place.
4. Place a rock in the middle of the sheeting. This causes the sheeting to form a funnel over the container. Condensation will be forced down into the container through this.

If a tube was inserted in step 2, you can drink straight from this container. Alternatively, you can collect the water and replace the container. This source can produce about 1 liter of water a day. Therefore, you cannot rely on this solely and need more sources of water.

Snow

Of course, snow is available during winter. However, it is possible to get snow in certain locations like the mountains all year round. Near the ocean in polar climates, icebergs can provide fresh water. If the ice is translucent and has a blue color, this is a sign that this is fresh water. Fresh water also splinters easily when stabbed with a knife. On the other hand, ice formed from salt water is opaque and gray.

Snow is simply frozen water, so all you must do is thaw this out. The next step is to purify this. Do not eat ice straight. Not only is this unhygienic, but it also causes dehydration because it lowers your body temperature and speeds up your metabolic rate to keep you warm.

To melt the snow, either mix it with other water you have or heat it. Even heating the snow requires the addition of some water, as it will scorch otherwise.

Condensation from metal in deserts

Condensation occurs on metal surfaces when there are wild variations in temperature, such as what occurs between day and night in deserts. This condensation will evaporate as soon as the sun comes out, so you need to catch it before then. Collect it on an absorbent cloth and wring this out. Repeat as needed.

Off-grid water supply systems

As an off-gridder, you have already located your water supply long before your home is built. If you're lucky enough, the land you have acquired provides this source. If not, you need to find an alternative. Even if your property does have a water source, you need to locate a backup. Your water supply can become polluted in a variety of such as:

- Wastewater or sewage
- Industrial waste
- Littering and jumping
- Acid rain

- The ruination of the surrounding ecosystem
- Disease

Emergencies do happen. Industrialization and advances in technology have made it so that pollution is a reality that we face in all forms, even in ways not listed above. The fact of the matter is your primary water source may be cut off. A backup for the backup is advisable, but let's start with getting at least two sources of water for your off-grid property.

Apart from digging a well and collecting rainwater, as mentioned before, you have the following options:

Public/City water

City water can be accessed if you live close enough to the city. But I would not advise this as a primary source of water. Just like water on your own property, city water is susceptible to emergencies, including pollution. This is a fact even though public water is regulated. It is a regular situation for city water to be cut off after storms because infrastructural issues cause problems in the supply distribution. If a catastrophe occurs, this is likely one of the first sources to be cut off. More often, it is more susceptible to pollution and contamination. The other options mentioned are more viable.

Wind energy to supply your home with water

Often, to get running water from a supply like a well or a pond to your home, you will need some sort of power supply. Wind turbines are a great option in windy, flat environments. A satisfactory wind speed is between 12 and 18 km per hour. Obstacles such as buildings and trees are removed from the site where the windmill is installed to ensure the wind reaches the fans.

Even outside of those conditions, you can buy a wind power kit to install a wind-powered water pump. There are several options available, including small wind electric generators known as aerogenerators and hybrids of wind and solar power systems, besides your traditional windmill. The typical windmill pumps between 1000 and 8000 liters of water per hour. The exact volume is dependent on the wind speed, the size of the pump cylinder, the elevation to which the water needs to be pumped, the type of windmill used, and the depth of the water body. Most windmills are capable of pumping water up to a depth of 60 meters at the average wind speed mentioned above.

One of the greatest advantages of using windmills in this way is that no fuel is required for them to be up and running. There are a few considerations when using windmills to supply your home with water. One of the biggest is the cost of setting up and maintaining the system. This can be quite high. An 8' tower costs upward of $3000. The cost itself includes not only the tower and frame of the windmill but also the cost of installation. You can DIY this, but I do not recommend it unless you have some expertise in that area. Far too many things can go wrong during installation. The towers are heavy - more than 350 pounds for an 8' tower - and accidents can happen. The cost of installation varies depending on factors like location and installation company pricing.

Additionally, the wind is a part of nature that cannot be controlled. It may be intermittent, and there is a need for a method of storage of the energy generated. As a result, the cost of batteries needs to be factored in.

Solar energy to supply your home with running water

This is best for environments with sunshine most of the year. A solar-powered water pump works by converting energy from the sun's rays into electricity, which is then used to pump water from the source to your homestead. The components of such a system include:

- Solar panels - Also called a solar photovoltaic system, this converts solar power into electricity.
- A water pump motor - This takes water from the source.

- An inverter - Water pumps run on alternating current (AC). The solar panels produce direct current (DC). The inverter is needed to convert DC to AC if the pump motor requires the conversion.
- Pipes - These are required to transport the water from the source to the ultimate location, which may be a storage system or directly to your homestead.
- Water tank - Tanks are needed to store water for times when there is no sunshine.
- Pump controllers - These regulate the water pump and protect it from power surges and motor damage if the water source dries up.

Using solar power to provide your home with water is an economically sound solution, eco-friendly, and useful in remote locations. They are also easy to install. This can be a DIY project that you take up as there are not too many mechanical parts. As such, the system is easy to maintain.

Hauling water into a large tank as a solid backup supply

You can manually fill up water tanks to use daily and to store for emergencies. This is not a good long-term solution - your back will certainly not appreciate it -

but can work until you sort out a more permanent answer.

Taking care of the plumbing

You need to find viable ways of bringing this water to your home not only to take care of your daily needs but also to store it for emergencies. Not only is it more convenient to have this set up, but it is also safer. Imagine having to haul water from a lake to your home in the middle of a storm, and you get my meaning.

Setting up an off-the-grid plumbing system should not be an option. It is a must. Choosing the right pipes for the job comes first. I recommend using PEX pipes. PEX stands for cross-linked polyethylene. These pipes are made of a flexible plastic material and are largely replacing traditional copper and galvanized steel pipes in newer construction projects. The flexibility allows PEX pipes to be connected to the main water control system as well as be run through walls and floors unin-terrupted to individual fixtures.

They are less expensive than copper pipes and do the task of transporting water to your home just as well. They can also be used to add a bit of flare to your home design as they come in different colors. These colors do hold significance though:

- Red PEX pipes are meant to carry hot water.
- Blue PEX pipes are meant to carry cold water.
- White and gray PEX pipes can carry either hot or cold water

The run length signifies the length of pipe you need to bring this water from the source to your home. Ensure that you have this figure correct. Do all measurements twice so that you cut your pipes only once. Cutting too long is a waste of time and cutting too short means wasting money as you need to replace the entire length. Luckily, PEX pipes come in several lengths. They range as short as 10-foot pieces, which are great for small repairs. They can also be as long as 500 feet. Such length allows for the installation of a home's entire water supply system. The pipes range from ⅜ to 1 inch in diameter.

The advantages of using PEX pipes include:

- PEX expands, which makes it resistant to freeze-cracking
- PEX does not erode, which means fewer chances of leaks and contamination of water PEX allows for water to flow silently, removing the hammering sound associated with metal pipes

- The color-coding system makes it easy to identify the hot and cold distribution
- PEX can be connected to the existing metal pipes when outfitted with the right fittings

There are a few cons to using PEX pipes, and they are:

- Currently, can't be recycled because it does not melt
- PEX needs special tools and connections for installation despite being DIY friendly
- Not suitable for outdoor use because UV rays destroy the structure of the piping

Before you install these pipes, you need to check your local building codes. It would not hurt to talk to an inspector first. This will save you the hassle and ensure you do the plumbing right on the first go.

Finally, test your water to figure out the quality. You risk getting sick from the use otherwise. Testing your water supply is not a complicated affair. Plenty of home water testing kits are available for purchase online and at physical stores. Test strips are one such test. To utilize this method of testing, fill a container with water from your supply and dip the test strip into it. After a few minutes, compare the color change noted on the strip with the chart included in the testing kit.

Alternatively, test the water supply by filling a container with water and adding a few drops of testing solution. Note the change in the water's color and compare it to the included chart.

Neither of these methods is superior to the other. They both provide an accurate measure of the hardness, chemicals present, pH, and chloride in your water supply. If you want a more comprehensive test that detects microorganisms, nitrates, and metals in water (and yes, I do recommend doing this test), contact an EPA-certified water testing service.

You have confirmed your water is safe to consume and use? Then, ensure that you set up a proper treatment system. Persons who are hooked up to city water should not (in a perfect world) need to set up a home treatment system. However, as you are the one responsible for monitoring the quality of your own water supply, this setup is a must. The system will improve the quality of water by reducing hazards and helping prevent odors and water hardness. Your typical water treatment system uses at least one or a combination of the 5 following methods:

Disinfection

This process kills harmful pathogens, worms, and more in a water supply. Methods of disinfection included pasteurization, UV light, boiling, and chlorination.

Filtration

Filtration removes solid particles suspended in the water supply, including sand, organic matter, and silt. Common filters include screening materials such as ceramic, fabric, and fibers. Mechanical filters can treat your entire house or supply since they can be mounted to a single water line or tap and even tank units. Filters need to be serviced regularly to ensure effectiveness. Other types of filters include:

- Neutralizing filters to treat acidic water.
- Oxidizing filters remove hydrogen sulfide (which causes a rotten egg smell), manganese, and iron. This is great for preventing water hardness.
- Activated carbon filters are great for removing unwanted tastes and odors from water.

Reverse osmosis

Pressurized, impure water passes through a semipermeable membrane to remove impurities during this process. The membrane's quality and the pressure determine the effectiveness of the removal of contaminants from the water.

Distillation

This process heats the water so that it evaporates and then condenses. The condensation is collected while undesirables such as pathogens, minerals, and solid substances are left behind. This is a daily process that has a capacity of between 2 and 5 gallons of treated water. About 5 gallons of water is required to produce 1 gallon of distilled water.

Ion exchange

Also called water softening, this removes the minerals from water that cause hardness. While it is not a health risk, hard water prevents the effective action of cleaning agents like soap and detergent and causes the buildup of scale in hot water pipes, water fixtures, and water heaters.

You can hire a plumber to set up all your water supply needs. However, you can also DIY this. Even if you outsource the main running of pipes, I think it is best to learn a few plumbing skills. You never know when you will be faced with a leak, and if you live in a remote location, getting a plumber to you at a moment's notice may be a hassle or impossible.

Learning to plumb is not difficult. You do not even need to do a formal course. The internet, books, and videos can provide you with the know-how. Just put some time and effort into learning.

Next, you must build a plumbing toolkit. The sky's the limit when it comes to what can be added to this. Screws. Spanners. The list goes on and on with infinite varieties of these tools, you can easily feel over-whelmed. But I implore you to take a breath. I got you! You do not need endless fancy tools, and you do not need many. You need just a few tools I will list below to get started:

- Sink auger
- Toilet auger
- Channel type pliers
- Plumber's tape
- Adjustable pipe wrench
- Faucet valve-seat wrench
- Tubing cutter
- Hacksaw
- Basin wrench
- Plunger

After these tools are in your kit, you can add more as needed.

Chapter Summary

Water is life. While the human body can go weeks without food, it only takes a few days to perish without water. Learning to spot the signs of possible water sources nearby and how to harness those sources is essential. But as an off-gridder, you must find viable ways of sourcing water and delivering it to your home.

Water is a must-have in your off-grid home, but so are other items. Let's look at these other essentials and how you can obtain them next.

11

SAVING YOUR FINDINGS

*L*ife is a risky business. That risk only increases when you choose to live outside of what is preached as the norm just as off-gridders do. Self-sufficiency and independence come part and parcel with living off the grid. This means knowing how to ensure your safety and good health even during an emergency. Preparedness is the name of the game to ensure this. This chapter shows you how to play the game with strategies for preserving food and water for emergency purposes.

Food

While it is possible to go for a few weeks without food, it is not a pleasant experience. The body can no longer regulate its temperature. Kidney function is impaired.

The immune system is weakened, and it is a lot easier to get sick. Metabolism slows down, and the body must rely on energy reserves to keep going. Vital organs and tissues are no longer supplied with the nutrition they need to work their best. The heart, ovaries, testes, lungs, and other organs shrink. Starvation is not on my list of recommendations. A zero-star rating, I would say.

Therefore, having adequate amounts of food on hand always is a sure way of ensuring you do not have to go through that horrendous ordeal. There are many ways of going about this and one is food preservation.

There will be times when you will end up having more food than you can possibly consume in a single go. Harvesting food from your garden is one such occurrence. Buying staple foods like rice, beans, and peas in bulk to keep more money in your pocket is another. To ensure the rest of your catch remains fit for consumption later, here comes food preservation techniques to the rescue. Popular methods of food preservation are:

Smoking

The typical image when we speak of smoking is of meats with complex flavors and juicy goodness. But so many other foods, such as poultry, seafood, grains, veggies, and even fruits, can be smoked at home using a gas grill or charcoal.

The basics of smoking are these:

- Low temperatures between 225°F to 300°F are used
- Cooking times are long, ranging from hours to days
- Smoke is created by distributing water-soaked chips, wood chunks, and (if you would like the extra flavor and smells) aromatics like fruit peels and fresh herbs over coals or in the smoker box of a gas grill. The wood smolders instead of bakes because of the low heat, and this gives the food its smoky flavor.
- The food is covered, so the smoke circulates, and the food cooks slowly.

The heat from smoking dehydrates food and makes it impossible for bacteria and similar microorganisms to grow. Wood smoke also has antimicrobial compounds that kill off what microbes the heat does not. A great thing about smoking is that you influence your food with unique flavors through aromatics and different types of wood. Common types of wood used for smoking include hickory, oak, pecan, maple, walnut, fruitwoods like cherry, apple, peach, plum, alder, and cedar.

There are two ways of smoking. The method used influences the final product achieved. Dry smoking uses the low heat of the smoldering wood to indirectly cook foods while infusing them with a smoky flavor. Wet smoking is more common. Also called water smoking, it uses a pan of water to maintain moisture and infuse food with tenderness. The humidity conditions help the smoke stick to the food to create a more intense flavor.

Salting

Salt prevents the growth of bacteria and other microbes by pulling moisture from food. Just like all living things, microbes need water to stay alive. As a result, salt is great for preserving foods such as meat, poultry, and fish. Even veggies can be salted for preservation. Depending on how much salt is used, salted food has the potential to last between a few months and several years. Because of the large amount of salt used, salted foods have a salty flavor, and some of this salt may need to be removed before consumption. This is done by allowing the salted food to soak in water for a few hours.

There are two ways to go about salt in food:

Dry curing

This salting method is popular when used to preserve charcuterie like sausage and ham. Cured meats can be used in soups, desserts, salads, entrees, and more. This was a classic method of preserving food historically, but it has seen a resurgence in the last few years. As such, cured meats are now commonly found in high-end restaurants, farmers' markets, and stores. You do not have to go to such locations when you can make your taste buds sing in the comfort of your off-grid home.

Dry curing combines air drying with salt curing. Sometimes smoking is also incorporated, but that is dependent on the desired product and the type of meat. The food is surrounded by salt and left to dry in a cool place. It may be necessary to remove accumulated liquid periodically as the salt draws water out of the meat. These meats have the potential to last for 18 months.

Wet curing

A solution called brine is used in wet curing. A brine is simply made of salt dissolved in water. The food is then placed in the brine and left in a cool dry place for several days, weeks, or even months. Vegetables are a popular choice as they are pickled in such a solution.

New flavors can be introduced by adding spices to the brine.

Drying/dehydration

This specific process uses an appliance called a dehydrator to extract the moisture from food for preservation. If you want your food to dry as quickly as possible with as little fuss as possible. The appliance is equipped with a temperature gauge, a timer, and fans for the even distribution of heat. They are also equipped with multiple trays to allow dehydration of more than one type of food at a time.

While dehydrators are efficient, they can be quite pricey, though. It is possible to get dehydrators for about $50. However, the quality of your dehydrator affects the quality of the final product. Higher-end options can cost up to $1,000.

Luckily, there are other methods of drying food. They include oven and solar drying. As the name suggests, oven drying uses an oven. A temperature of around 140° F (60° C) (or slightly less) is used to dry the food for an average of 6 to 10 hours, depending on the specific type of food. Higher temperatures will cook the food instead of dry it. While drying the food in the oven, prop the door open slightly so that extra moisture escapes.

This is the most energy-efficient method of drying. Solar dehydrators use the power of the sun to dry foods. There is no need to use electricity or gas. This device can be purchased, but it can also be DIYed using inexpensive materials sourced at your local hardware store. You can get a simple plan to build this with a Google search along with a list of materials that can include plywood, a screen to keep bugs out, screws, and a plexiglass cover.

The best foods to dehydrate include:

- Lean meats and poultry like chicken, beef, and fish.
- Fruits like bananas, apples, and mangoes. Vegetables like cabbage, eggplant, and mushrooms.
- Herbs like rosemary, thyme, mint, and lavender
- Sauces and syrups like pizza sauce, barbecue sauce, molasses, and jam

Foods that are high in oil or fat are not appropriate for drying.

Foods need to be prepped before dehydrating. For example, fruits and veggies need to be thinly sliced and then placed in a single layer until they become crisp. Meats, fish, and poultry need to either be cooked, roasted, or steamed between 160° F (71° C) and 165°F (74° C) before being dried to ensure food-borne illnesses do not develop. Properly dried foods last between a few months and a few years.

Cold storage

Freezing foods at 0°F prevents the growth and repro-duction of microorganisms that cause food-borne diseases. Ideally, freezers should be kept at -10°F. Deep freezers can freeze items in an off-grid home if the electricity supply is steady. However, to be more conservative and less reliant on electricity, a root cellar may be used.

Preserving food in a root cellar is a method of cold storage as it relies on cooling, insulation, and humidi-fying processes to keep food fresh. Root cellars were used to preserve foods using lower temperatures decades ago when refrigerators were not so popular, but today, they are becoming - pardon my pun - cool again. They were used mainly to preserve fruits and veggies. While it is great to have a dedicated space like the root cellars described in Chapter 8, any storage location that uses the earth's insulation, natural cooling, and humidity can be deemed a root cellar. I have seen people use an old refrigerator that no longer works as a root cellar by installing it into the ground.

Pickling and fermentation

Unlike most other preservation methods that rely on removing water from the food item, pickling and fermentation rely on the antimicrobial actions of vinegar. Vinegar contains acids such as lactic or acetic acid. This acid changes the chemical structure of microbes, thus killing them. All you must do is ensure your food is submerged in a vinegar solution to preserve food in this way. Be mindful that the appearance, texture, and taste of the food will change.

The basic items you need to begin your pickling and fermentation journey are:

- 1 quart Mason jars
- Sealable lids
- Sea salt
- Water

You can also add herbs and seasoning to customize this taste. The naturally occurring bacteria in fruit and vegetables called lactobacillus will convert the sugars in the fruit and vegetables into lactic acid so that the food gains its characteristic sour or tangy flavor. This occurs over a few days. Fermented foods last between 4 and 18 months. Check for edibility by looking for signs of mold or color changes. As long as there is none, the fermented food is good to eat.

Cold box

This is a simplified refrigeration technique that keeps food cold. Most microbes cannot survive in cold conditions.

Other traditional methods

- Other methods of food preservation are, but are not limited to:
- Coating the food with non-rancid fat candying in honey
- Covering the food in ashes

I encourage you to do a bit of research on these food preservation methods and others to find the ones that suit your lifestyle best.

Water

Water is life. At no time can you go without it for an extended period. Therefore, you need to not only have a primary supply but also backup methods of gaining water for hydration, sanitation, and more.

Cleaning and preserving water

As much as water is needed to ensure that the body performs optimally, drinking any water found is a recipe for disaster. The World Health Organization reports that nearly half a million people die of water-borne illnesses yearly. If that statistic is not dismal enough, millions more are sickened due to contaminated water annually. Drinking polluted water increases the risk of contracting infections like diarrhea, cholera, dysentery, typhoid, and polio. These conditions are potentially deadly.

Therefore, it must be stressed that clean water is life.

The municipal water supply may be insufficient or even absent with off-grid living. As such, finding and supplying your home with clean drinking water can be a serious issue. Luckily, contaminated water can be saved with basic purification techniques that remove impurities and make the liquid drinkable.

These techniques include:

Boiling

This is a tried-and-true method of purifying water as most microbes cannot live in temperatures that exceed 170°F. Water boils at 212°F at sea level and 200°F at higher elevations. The water needs to be bubbling for at least 2 minutes, as it boils to effectively kill pathogens. You do not need any special equipment to boil water apart from a heat source and a pan. Unfortunately, boiling water can be time-consuming, as you can only boil limited amounts of water at a time. You also must wait for the finished product to cool down before drinking.

Filters

Filters are inexpensive, light, and packable. They not only remove solid particles from the water but also bacteria if their pore size is small enough. The amount of water that can be filtered at a time is small. Also, filters do not kill viruses.

UV devices

Such devices include sterilization pens. All you must do is stir the water with the device for 1 to 2 minutes, and it becomes drinkable. They are light and portable. They need batteries to operate and do not remove sediments like silt or mud.

Disinfecting tablets

These tablets contain compounds like Iodine and Chlorine Dioxide. They kill water-borne microbes. They are light to pack, easy to use, and inexpensive. Unfortunately, these do not remove solid particles like mud. They change the taste of water, and you need to allow them 30 minutes to work their magic before you drink the water.

Iodine disinfecting tablets must not be used by pregnant women and people suffering from thyroid conditions.

Other methods of water purification include:

- Distillation, which relies on heat to evaporate water (produce steam). Solid particles and microbes are left behind. The evaporated water is collected and is safe to use. Distillation can sound like a complicated process, but it can be performed easily at home. All you must do is boil water so that it turns to vapor. As the vapor condenses back to liquid water, it leaves behind any unwanted residue.
- Solar water disinfection uses sunlight to purify water. This is a free method that does not use chemicals, but it does not guarantee that the water is safe.
- Survival straws can be used as you would a normal straw. As water is drawn through the tube, it is filtered to remove contaminants.
- Household chemicals, namely chlorine bleach. You only need two drops per gallon of water for this strategy to work.

Stockpiling water for survival

You have left the city life several miles behind you and have chosen the open land to live your remaining years in harmony. Though there are a lot of differences between these two living styles, some things never change – like the need for basics like water.

While the cities are burgeoning with creative water filtration and storage solutions, there are still limited means to store water in the countryside. You need to develop your own means of storing water. But you got this. I am here to help. I will provide you with a few ways that you can store water using natural means that work especially well if you're facing emergency conditions.

Wooden container

A thick branch or dry log will create this kind of container. Char the wood over an open fire and scrape the charred pieces to form a depression in the wood. Sand the hole that you have created for a smooth surface, and you're all set with the impromptu container.

Never use cracked or rotted wood for this.

Birch bark

The pliable nature of birch bark lets you create holding containers. This characteristic only increases when you heat the material.

Bamboo

Bamboo can be crafted into cups and bowls to hold water by sealing one end of a piece. An added a is the water can be a source of water as the liquid flows through its hollow stems.

Animal parts

Some animals' bladders, intestines, and skin can function as makeshift water containers if you're pressed for a way to hold the water. These need to be cleaned thoroughly. The lining must be scraped off, and the structure may be boiled to remove any nasty microbes lying in wait. Then all you have to do is tie one end to keep the water from spilling out and fill up.

More containers

Nature has no shortage of water to help you, including to contain water. All you must do is be resourceful and look at things in a new light. Coconut shells, hollowed-out acorns, seashells, turtle shells... All of these can hold water under the right circumstances.

Chapter Summary

Prepare for possible emergencies by preserving food and water. Preservation techniques like smoking and salting allow you to use foods that you cannot consume today, weeks, months, and even years later. Make sure that water is always safe to drink by purifying it with methods like boiling and filtering.

The next chapter explores different options for powering your off-the-grid home.

12

POWERING UP YOUR OFF-GRID HOME

e have spoken about generating your own power as an off-gridder. That is quite appropriate since that is the one utility where you must disconnect from the traditional source of power and supply your own to earn the title of off-gridder. This self-sufficiency is liberating. It is a feeling that over 180,000 American families already enjoy, and you can feel it too. This chapter dives into more specifics about some of the most popular ways of generating your own power, such as the benefits and drawbacks, and finally gives you the method of how to get started on installing these in your off-grid home.

Methods of generating electricity

Solar energy, wind energy, and micro-hydro energy are the most popular methods of off-grid power. That is so because they allow users a renewable, fully independent way of powering their homes without leaving a carbon footprint. You do not have power bills draining your wallet at the end of every month. Some instances may allow you to supply electricity companies with the excess you generate for a fee. Talk about flipping the coin! You also have peace of mind, safe from the worry that this utility infrastructure will collapse at any time.

You also have to consider the possible cons of generating your own power. The biggest of these is the cost. Simple system setups put a hole of tens of thousands of dollars into your bank account. There is also the cost of maintaining these systems and covering any repairs needed. The comfort in this is knowing that savings in utilities will eventually make up for this upfront cost.

The next disadvantage is that options for using these sustainable sources of energy are limited based on location. You may even need to combine sources of energy as conditions may not last all year to allow utilization of one source. No matter what, a back source of power is required, but the same can be said for relying on the electricity company.

Let's look at the pros and cons of using the most popular ways off-gridders generate power:

Solar energy

This is the most sought-after way of generating power by off-gridders. The harnessing of this type of power requires the use of photovoltaic panels just as with supplying your home with water using solar-powered pumps. They convert light from the sun into electricity. Most places on this planet receive sunlight, so this method's popularity comes from having the least number of special criteria to be viable.

Solar panels are the first item needed to ensure the correct functioning of this system. But how many do you need?

The average home in the US consumes more than 10,000 kWh of energy every year. To meet that demand, between 30 and 35 250-watt solar panels need to be installed to generate enough electricity to power such a home. To arrive at the number of solar panels you need to power your home. Go through this process:

- Calculate your electricity consumption in kWh. You can use your previous electricity bills to average this. Of course, in your off-the-grid home, you expect to use less electricity than this. You can guess this average based on your off-grid property's appliances, fittings, fixtures, and other electricity needs. You can use this free annual electricity consumption calculator linked here to help with this: https://www.energy.gov/energysaver/estimating-appliance-and-home-electronic-energy-use.

- Divide your electricity consumption by the solar panel production estimate. This varies from location to location and from property to property. Arizona (1.31) and Maine (1.61) have the highest and lowest production ratios in the US. Use this range as your guide.
- Divide the number arrived at in the step above by 250, which is the wattage average of a single solar panel. This will provide a good gauge of how many solar panels will completely power your home.

Let's illustrate this with an example. The calculation for a home will use 12.000 kWh of electricity annually. This home is in Texas, which has a production ratio of 1.31. The math looks like this:

12,000 kWh of annual electricity usage / 1.31 = 9,160.3
9,160.3 / 250 = 36.6 panels

Rounding this number off, you will see the number of panels needed is 37.

Solar power might be the least cost-effective method when comparing the high cost of equipment needed to harness this energy versus the output. With that being said, it needs to be noted that the cost of harnessing solar energy to power homes is falling. Solar prices have decreased by almost 35% in Texas between 2014 and 2019. Other places in the United States have seen more dramatic decreases, with some experiencing a lowered cost of solar panel installation by as much as 70% between 2009 and 2019. This has helped the demand for the installation of residential solar panels and the use of solar power in general to rise.

Users also need to consider that cloudy periods, and nighttime are limitations when it comes to power generation. While the sunlight doesn't have to be blazing hot to generate power, the sunnier it is, the more power is generated. Batteries are used to store power while it is generated, so you do not have to worry about it being dark during the night or days with less sunlight. Excess electricity generated can be sold to the nation's grid as part of SEG (the Government's Smart Export Guarantee). This allows you to get a return on your investment in this type of renewable energy.

Wind energy

Wind power costs less to set up compared to solar power and so the cost-effectiveness is higher. Output is gained when the wind moves through installed wind turbines. The turbines spin and produce electricity.

Unfortunately, many locations are not windy enough to make this a good investment. Also, a large, open area is needed to do the setup. Even if the location is windy, if the wind doesn't move in a consistent direction, the turbines will not work as necessary to generate electricity.

If wind power is not an issue and you decide to take the plunge into setting up wind turbines to power your off-grid home, a planning phase is needed. The steps involved are:

- Estimating the wind resource, you have available. This is the average annual wind speed at the site where you plan to erect the wind turbines. Means by which you can gain this information include accessing airport wind speed data, vegetation flagging, which is noting the effect of strong winds on vegetation in the area, gaining data from a local small wind system, and directly monitoring the wind resource with a measuring system. The last measure can cost between $600 and $1200 to set up. An area suitable for setting up wind power must have an average annual wind speed of at least 9 miles per hour. This is equivalent to 4 meters per second.

- Gaining the permits and zoning requirements needed to set up your wind energy system.
- Creating a cost analysis of setting up the system.

With the plan in place, you can move on to installing the system. The first step is finding the best location to set this up. This process is called siting. A professional installer should help you with this. This person will help you note wind resource considerations such as the complexity of the terrain in the installation site, whether you will be accessing wind from the gully or leeward side on hilly terrain, and plans for possible future obstructions like trees that haven't yet reached their full height and new buildings. Wind turbines need to be situated at least 30 feet higher than any structure within 300 feet.

System considerations will also be discussed with this professional. For the best experience with generating wind power, only use small wind turbines that have been tested and certified to meet safety standards and national performance. You also need to lower and raise the wind turbine tower when it is time for maintenance. The load that the wind turbines will carry such as your home, storage in batteries, water pumps, and more need to be taken into consideration. These are only a few of the thoughts that need to be at the forefront of your mind when installing wind turbines, and that is why I recommended the use of a professional installation company.

With an estimate of the system's output, you can choose the right size small wind turbine and tower to install. The residential application of small wind turbines typically ranges in size between 400 watts and 20 kilowatts. This depends on the amount of electricity generated. The typical home uses 10,000 kWh of electricity every year. This totals almost 900 kWh every month. If you plan to match this demand, then a wind turbine that is rated between 5 kWh and 15 kWh is needed. This might be lower depending on the electricity needs of your off-grid home. The size needed will also depend on the annual average wind speed. Where there are higher annual average wind speeds, smaller-sized wind turbines are adequate.

Factors that affect animal energy output included:

- The frequency distribution of the wind at the site. This describes the estimated number of hours the wind blows at particular speeds each year.

- The wind turbine's power curve.
- The height of the tower of the wind turbine.

Wind is a free resource. If you believe the pros outweigh the cons and install a wind turbine, after the initial cost of installation and maintenance, the cost of your electricity will go down drastically. You will leave a lesser carbon footprint by using a renewable energy source. You also do not have to worry if you have a few calm days at the site as batteries can be used for electricity storage.

Micro-hydro energy

Just like wind energy, harnessing micro-hydro energy makes use of spinning turbines. The difference is that electricity is generated by the motion of water spinning through turbines. This type of power gives you the most bang for your buck based on the cost of setup versus output. This is one of the simplest power systems you can set up, and it seriously needs to be considered if you have flowing water on your property. Lots of farmers and ranchers have made use of micro-hydro power systems.

To determine if micro-hydro energy is right for you, estimate the amount of power that you will gain from a flowing water site. This includes the calculation of two components:

1. The head, which is the vertical distance the waterfalls
2. The flow, which is the quantity of water flowing

Use the following calculation to determine the estimated output:

$$[\text{net head (feet)} \times \text{flow (GPM)}] \div 10 = W \text{ (Power or Watts)}$$

A micro-hydropower system needs to produce between 50% and 70% efficiency to validate the installation. Permits and water rights are also necessary to set up this system on your property, so seek these out before installation.

A small hydropower system can generate as much as 100 kilowatts of electricity. However, a 10-kilowatt micro-hydropower system is usually enough to power an entire large home. In fact, it can power a small resort or a hobby farm.

The components of a micro-hydro energy system include:

- The water conveyance is a pipeline or channel that delivers the water to the next component.
- A waterwheel, pump, or turbine to transform the energy produced by the flowing water into rotational energy.
- A generator or alternator transforms this rotational energy into electricity.
- A regulator to control the generator
- Electrical wiring to deliver the electricity to your home and other sites where it is needed.

Just like with solar energy, an inverter may be needed to convert direct current into alternating current. You can avoid this cost by buying household appliances that run on direct current.

Several options for turbines exist. First and foremost, there are impulse turbines, which have the least complex design and rely on the velocity of the water to move the wheel. Next, there are reaction turbines, which are more complex but highly efficient. They rely on pressure instead of velocity to produce energy. These are used in more large-scale operations because of the complexity and higher cost.

The drawback to this source of energy is that few places on earth have enough water volume and related conditions that allow the output of energy that makes sense to go through with such an installation.

Installing the backup power

There are several reasons why any of the above-mentioned energy sources could stop working. It may be a rainy day, and so the solar power is out. It may be that the area is going through a dry spell and the source of water is running low, meaning less or no output from the micro-hydro energy. The wind is free, but you have no control over it, and it can stop blowing at any time. These occurrences can be unpredictable, and so you need to always be prepared for them. You want to ensure that your life is interrupted as little as possible by them. A backup energy source is your savior.

The options for this include:

1. Batteries
2. Generators

The most common backup energy source currently is a generator. The options for these include those that run on fuel sources like propane, diesel, and gasoline. Further options include three-phase, single-phase, and inverter generators. The sizes of these are widely varied from as little as 5 watts to higher power outputs, like 5 kilowatts.

Some are portable, but it is better if this is in a permanent space when used as backup power for your homestead. A generator should never be used in enclosed spaces like inside your home, a garage, or a shed as this develops a risk for carbon monoxide poisoning.

The right option can give a large enough energy output to power your entire home while your main source of power is out of commission. It is best to commission the services of a licensed electrician to install the generator to avoid the risk of electrocution, electric shock, carbon monoxide poisoning, and fires.

A few tips for installing a backup generator in a permanent location are:

- Place this on a precast concrete slab that is compacted into the ground
- Secure the generator in place with bolts drilled into the concrete slab
- Ensure that the generator is installed more than 5 feet away from doors and windows
- Do not set up the generator in humid conditions
- Ensure the cables used are suitable for the environment.
- Unwind the power cables when operating a generator as coiled cables can become

quite hot.

- Do not operate generators near combustible materials
- If you are using a fuel-powered generator, store the extra fuel in a separate location and only refuel a generator after it has sufficiently cooled

Fuel-powered generators have dominated the market for backup power supplies for a very long time. However, there are a few downsides to using fuel-powered generators. They can be noisy. They need to be maintained. They require a fuel source. They pose a hazard in the form of electric shock, fires, and carbon monoxide poisoning. They are not the most eco-friendly device. Many people look for a solution that does not have these drawbacks, and battery banks have come to the rescue.

Even when connected to your typical grid, many people use batteries to protect their appliances from power surges and other power-related issues. If there is a surge or outage, the battery power instantly kicks into power appliances for a period. When using battery banks, the concept is simple - several batteries are connected to create one big battery, hence the name battery bank.

To create a battery bank, you need the following items:

- Batteries, the sizes of which will be determined by your household needs
- An inverter or charger
- battery cables
- An inline fuse
- A battery rack
- Electrical wiring

There are a few other bits and bobs that go into the installation of this, but these are the basics. Installing a battery bank can be a DIY project after much research, but it is better to contract the services of a qualified electrician. Placing one wire in the wrong location or creating one wrong connection can burn your off-grid house to the ground within minutes, so it is better to take up this expense.

While a battery bank can power your entire home for some time, it is not practical to rely on this for an extended amount of time. It simply will not hold up. Therefore, it is best to only connect the battery bank in such a way that it only takes up critical loads until the primary source of power is restored. Do not hook up appliances like air conditioners that demand a lot of electricity to this. Use 4 to 8 smaller circuits to power the essentials like communication, lighting, refrigeration, and convenience outlets. Batteries that can power more than this load are expensive.

Generators are the most cost-efficient even though they need an upfront investment. On the other hand, batteries are more versatile and do not need to be maintained. Which one is the right backup power supply for your off-the-grid home? Weigh the pros and cons against your needs, and then you can decide.

Chapter Summary

Solar energy, wind energy, and micro-hydro energy are the most popular methods of off-grid power. They are renewable, allow full independence from electricity companies, are cost-efficient, and leave no carbon footprint.

Drawbacks to using these sustainable sources of energy include the cost, which ranges into tens of thousands of dollars. Maintenance and repairs also cost a pretty penny. But the savings in utilities will eventually make up for this upfront cost.

It must also be noted that these sources of energy are location dependent.

A backup energy source such as a gas generator must be installed for instances when the main source of power is nonfunctional.

The next utility we will explore is a sewage system.

13

TAKING CARE OF HEALTH & HYGIENE

*O*ff-grid living is too often likened to the image of people living in unsanitary conditions.

People who have approached living off-the-grid with a plan for keeping proper hygiene and sanitation live with anything but this misconception. They are just as clean and healthy as people who live on the grid, maybe even more so since they have given up the polluted air and other conditions that are considered a normal part of that environment.

The words 'hygiene' and 'sanitation' are often used interchangeably. While they can be considered cousins, they are not one and the same. Hygiene refers to the acts that you perform to keep clean and healthy. We have all the modern convenience that makes these behaviors easy in modern society. Maintaining good hygiene might not come as easily as living off-the-grid, but neither is good hygiene a sacrifice that you must make. All you must do is find alternatives to do the same tasks.

There are different types of hygiene. There is personal hygiene, food hygiene, domestic hygiene, and environmental hygiene. As we know, keeping your person clean and healthy does no good if you do not do the same with the environment where you live or the standards that you use to feed, clothe and house yourself. Ways that you can practice good hygiene overall include:

- Gather the hygiene essentials and create stockpiles such as a dental kit, bathing kit, cleaning kit, feminine hygiene products, and more. Make sure that you have the products needed to maintain the high standard that you have set for caring for yourself and your environment.
- Practice safe measures, such as frequent hand washing and cleaning up after yourself promptly.
- Clean and store the edibles properly. This ensures food does not spoil, which can lead to food poisoning if you eat them, an infestation

by rodents and insects, both of which spread diseases.

- DO NOT drink water from unreliable sources
- Keep your meds handy and in a safe, clean environment.
- Educate yourself on natural remedies to avoid relying overly on pharmaceutical sources to treat ailments.

Going hand in hand with hygiene is sanitation. Sanitation refers to the behaviors that encompass good hygiene as well as facilities that enable these behaviors. Therefore, besides practicing habits that ensure you are clean and healthy, you also need to set up the space and provision to allow you to upkeep these practices.

Sanitation is necessary to:

- Prevent the development and spread of sickness and disease in households.
- Increase self-esteem and self-confidence as how we view ourselves is partly shaped by hygiene and sanitation.
- Promote good mental health. Cluttered and untidy environments lead to cluttered thinking and poor emotional well-being. By extension, good sanitation increases concentration and productivity.

- Improved quality of life overall.

Types of sanitation systems and how to build them

Depending on how far off-the-grid you go, you are likely to disconnect yourself from the modern sewage system, a significant sanitation facility. In urban environments, we take for granted the vital role that this system plays in keeping us safe, healthy, and clean.

Just as with any other type of utility, an emergency can mean that the sewage system can be shut off. As an off-gridder, even if you are within the reach of the municipal sewage system, gaining independence is something to consider. That consideration begins with knowing what your options are.

Pit latrine

Also called an outhouse, long drop, or pit toilet, this is the easiest sanitation system that you can develop on your off-the-grid property. It allows for the collection of human urine and feces in a hole dug into the ground. All you have to do is dig a deep hole that is at least 5 feet deep and 4 feet wide. Sometimes, a concrete slab is placed over it along with a seat toilet or a squat. Ensure your privacy by building a shelter around it, and you're almost all set to go. The minimum amount of installation material and low labor costs that go into constructing this sanitation system make it low-cost. They do not require a great deal of expertise to construct, and almost any able-bodied person can create one. The advantages of creating a pit latrine include:

- They do not require the installation of water systems, and so they are appropriate in areas where there is no water supply.
- The excreta can be drained, degraded, and transformed into nutrient-rich material that can be used to improve the quality of soil used for gardening.
- They are easy to clean and keep if properly constructed slabs are installed.

There are also a few disadvantages. This list includes:

- Pit latrines can become a breeding ground for mosquitoes and flies if not properly constructed or sealed off.
- Foul odors are emitted from the pit.
- A new pit needs to be dug every time one becomes filled.
- It is not suitable for children to use a pit latrine if a slab has not been installed or if the hole is too big.

If you decide a pit latrine is a good option for you, a few considerations need to be made to ensure that this remains safe and healthy for you to use.

The first consideration is the location you placed this. It should never be placed uphill from a water source such as a well or a lake. Consider your neighbor's water sources, too. The water source is likely to become contaminated if you ignore this rule. This happens most readily in areas where the rocks are fissured, such as in limestone areas. Even if the latrine is downhill from the water source, it must be at least 30 yards away.

Other considerations include ensuring that the pit is built above flood level and that the structure is closed off when it is not in use. This ensures that insects such as flies do not take up residence. When the latrine becomes at least one-and-a-half feet filled to the top, it should be covered up with soil.

Human waste produces methane gas, and a buildup of this can cause an explosion if there is an exposed flame in proximity. Therefore, you should never smoke or drop lit matches in a latrine.

There are a few variations of the simple pit latrine described above. The simple pit latrine is composed of three major parts:

1. A hole in the ground
2. A concrete slab with a small hole carved in. The concrete slab is used where the soil may be unstable and to prevent the pit from collapsing in on itself.
3. A shelter

The hole should be covered to contain the smells and to prevent flies. When the hole is filled, a new hole is dug, and the shelter and slab can be reused in the new area. The following variations build on the foundation set by the simple version.

The ventilated improved pit (VIP) latrine

The major difference between this type of pit latrine and the simple version is the management of odors. Instead of using a lid over the hole, a vertical ventilation pipe is installed to remove odors. A mesh covering is placed over the pipe to ensure flies are kept out.

The twin-pit ventilated latrine

This version builds on the concept of the ventilated pit described above. Two pits with squat holes are dug next to each other. With the shelter covering both holes. Only one hole is used at a time while the other is closed. Once one hole is filled, it is sealed, allowing its contents to be used as manure about a year after. The ventilation pipe is moved to whichever space houses the hole currently in use.

The pour-flush latrine

This pit latrine introduces the use of water for flushing. A unique pan cast is used in the slab cover above the pit in such a latrine. It is used to contain smells. The pit is positioned either directly below the hole or offset in another close location. The latrine shelter can be inside the home while the pit is outside. Offset pits need to be outfitted with a pipe between the pit and the pan to allow water to flush. This can be modified to have a twin pit like the above.

The composting latrine

This type of pit latrine is specifically created to develop soil fertilizer for gardening. The pit is watertight, and ash, brown matter, and green matter are added to the pit after every use. If the moisture content and the chemical balance within the pit is controlled, the contents can be used as fertilizer within a few months.

NO MATTER how sophisticated you get with the design, many people are not thrilled about having to go outside (with most variations of the latrine) to use toilet facilities and this leads us to the next sanitation system options.

Compost toilet

A more up-to-date option for a sanitation system is a compost toilet. The benefits of this type of system are numerous. It does not create pollution. It allows your waste to be composed so that bigger, more bountiful plants grow in your garden. Compost toilets are a great solution where plumbing is not practical and to maximize the use of water in areas where water is scarce. You need very little to no water to make use of a compost toilet.

You have several options when it comes to utilizing this sanitation system. The simplest form of a compost toilet involves doing your business over a bucket that has been fitted with a toilet seat. Cover the dropping with sawdust or other similar carbon material after every use. When the bucket is filled, place the contents into your compost heap and cover it with more sawdust. Be mindful that you should use separate buckets for number 1 and number 2. Urine can safely be dumped into your yard as it is sterile unless in rare cases such as if a person suffers from a kidney infection.

This system comes with some concerns, such as the possible odors produced and needing a steady supply of sawdust. That is not something that you necessarily have to worry about. Composting toilets have a significantly lower chance of producing a foul order, especially compared to a pit latrine. Composting of human waste is done with bacteria that are under aerobic conditions. This means this is an oxygen-free environment. The processes facilitated by oxygen cause the odor. As such, the waste tends to give off an odorless compost that is safe to use in agricultural practices.

You can set up a neat system with tools that can easily be sourced at the hardware store. For a DIY system, you need:

- 2 5-gallon buckets that are the same height (one to use after the other is filled)
- 4 2x4 pieces of wood that are the same height as the buckets
- A toilet seat and its accompanying hardware A piece of plywood that is slightly larger than the toilet seat
- 8 screws

With these few simple steps, you can have your compost toilet set up in a few minutes:

1. Create a hole the same size as the bucket in the piece of plywood.
2. Line the toilet seat up to cover the hole just created

3. Mark then drill the holes to attach the toilet seat
4. Screw on a 2x4 on each corner of the plywood to create legs
5. Flip the plywood over, so it stands on the legs
6. Attach the toilet seat to the plywood using the previously drilled holes
7. Place one bucket so that it is filled under the hole in the plywood
8. Add a few inches of sawdust

That's it! You're all done. You can dress this construction up or down if it suits you better.

The solution is to buy a modern composting toilet. They are up there in price, but most people consider them worth it. They have vent hoses, so they are odorless, and they compost much faster.

DIY septic tank

This last sanitation system is the most sophisticated and the costliest to set up. A septic tank is a device created from steel, concrete, or fiberglass. It is installed underground, away from the main house. The location chosen is usually to the back or the side of the property. Flushing toilets and sinks (inside the house or at other locations on the property) are connected to this. Every time a toilet is flushed, or a sink is used, the water and human waste from the devices are directed to the septic tank via underground pipes. The water and waste are separated in the septic tank. The water is released from the tank systematically into the surrounding soil. The waste is collected in the tank and will be pumped out as scheduled for periodic maintenance. This timeframe is typically every 3 to 5 years. Additionally, the mechanical components and other parts of the system should be inspected at the same time.

Septic tank installation is becoming more popular because of the many benefits of the setup. Such advantages include:

Environmental friendliness

Septic tanks remove bacteria from the water before releasing the liquid into the soil. This means that water supplies and sources nearby will not become contaminated.

Cost-effectiveness

While septic tanks are more expensive to set up compared to the other 2 sanitation systems outlined above, they are far less expensive compared to setting up expensive sewer lines. In the long term, you get much bang for your buck along with less hassle.

Durability

Septic tanks rarely need to be replaced if they are maintained correctly

Efficient water use

There needs to be an awareness of how much water is being used if you use a septic tank. The system can become easily overwhelmed if too much water is used. The same applies if non-food items are dumped into the septic tank.

Some people may see this as a disadvantage, but I see it as an advantage since it encourages more responsibility and efficient use of water.

There are a few cons to the system, and this list includes:

Drains can become backed up

Most often, septic tank drains have become clogged when items that should not be flushed or dumped into the system are placed there. Signs that your drains may be backed up include slow-flushing toilets as well as sinks and tubs that are slow to drain. Call in a plumber to inspect the system if you suspect a backed-up drain.

The need for periodic maintenance

The cost of having a septic tank pumped every 3 to 5 years ranges between $200 and $400 per period. If this periodic maintenance is not upheld, you risk having your drains becoming backed up, which only increases your expenses.

The need for replacement

Septic tanks need to be replaced every 20 to 40 years. The cost for this depends on a few factors, like the size of the septic tank and the location, but you can expect to spend between $3,000 and $10,000 for this.

The possibility of ruptured pipes

The pipes of your septic system can become ruptured for several reasons, such as an earthquake, a vehicle rolling over them, and roots invading the space. When this happens, the wastewater leaks into the soil, and foul odors are emitted. The ground also becomes mushy. For the maintenance of good health and safety, ruptured pipes must be replaced immediately.

The septic tank is composed of two parts. The first part is a tank that holds and digests the waste. The next part is the dispersal field, where waste is automatically filtered into. Just like a model composting toilet, users do not have to deal with odors. This is more familiar to most people, as it more closely resembles the municipal sewage system. You can have a full-blown toilet and bathroom as typically seen in cities with this setup.

A septic tank not only accepts wastewater from your toilets and bathroom, but also from the washing machine and garbage disposal. The solid particles sink to the bottom of the tank while the liquids are excreted into the dispersal field. There are a few important terms that you need to be familiar with to ensure the proper running of your septic system:

Inspection ports

These can come in the form of pipes. They allow cameras and other small tools to fit into the space. They also allow a minimal look into the tank. All of this ensures the proper function of the tank.

Manhole

Big enough to allow someone to climb into. This is the hole at the top of the septic tank.

Effluent

Also called wastewater, this is the liquid that leaves the septic tank and goes into the dispersal field.

Scum

This is the accumulation of oil or grease at the top of the wastewater in the septic tank. It floats, but special compartments and outlets prevent the scum from leaving the tank. Only liquids are permitted into the dispersal field.

Sludge

This is the solid waste that settles in the bottle of the tank. During maintenance, you may be advised to use biological additives that increase the number of helpful bacteria and enzymes in the tank. They break these particles down. The additives can increase the time needed between tank pumps.

Drain field

Also called a leach field, this is the area where wastewater flows into the tank. The soil there is unsaturated and filters the harmful pathogens from the wastewater.

The septic system requires the input of water and plumbing to be set up to facilitate the transfer of waste from the toilet to the system.

Here are a few tips to ensure the smooth installation, use, and maintenance of a septic tank:

Get acquainted with your local laws and codes

Regulations surround the installation, replacement, and maintenance of septic tanks. Get acquainted with the specifics of the area you have chosen to go off-the-grid.

Schedule regular system inspections and maintenance

Inspections and maintenance of the septic system prevent you from encountering issues unnecessarily. A licensed inspector will ensure:

- There are no leaks or clogs
- The pipes uphold their integrity.
- Drainage and ventilation are optimal
- Alert you of issues you may encounter in the future (like roots rupturing your pipes), so you can mitigate these problems before they even arise.

It is easy for inspection and maintenance to slip from your mind, so do not leave it up to chance. Place reminders for those activities in your schedule.

Understand the specs of your septic system

The size septic tank you require is based on the number of bedrooms your home has. The minimum capacity for a home with no bedroom is 750 gallons. These tanks are being used less and less, and you will probably have a difficult time sourcing one.

The table below provides an excellent guide for determining the size septic tank you need:

No. of bedrooms in a home	Minimum septic tank capacity recommended	Minimum liquid surface area needed for septic tank
1-3	1,000 gallons	27 sq. ft.
4	1,200 gallons	34 sq. ft.
5	1,500 gallons	40 sq. ft.
6	1,750 gallons	47 sq. ft.

Be mindful that the size of the septic tank determines how often it needs to be pumped.

Chapter Summary

Hygiene is the collection of behaviors performed to keep clean and healthy. This does not just entail what you do to keep your person clean and healthy, but also your environment. Sanitation refers to good hygiene and the facilities that enable these behaviors. You can still have those facilities with off-grid-living. Options include building a pit latrine, compost toilet, and a septic tank.

The next chapter explores how to keep your home safe from different types of threats.

14

HOME, SECURE HOME

*O*ften, when we hear of a compromise in human safety, we think of human-to-human interactions or trying to make it to the other side of a disaster unscathed. But the threat to human safety encompasses more than those things. This chapter addresses what some of them are and how you can protect yourself from them off the grid.

Keeping safe from wild animals

Connecting with Mother Nature means likely connecting with the other animals that she has generously placed on earth. Sometimes that can be a great experience. There is nothing as majestic as seeing a wolf or a deer in its natural element. From afar, that is. But there is danger present when you share the same habitat with such creatures. As beautiful as they are from afar, up close they can pose great danger.

You can do the smart thing and stay away from them, but that does not remove the fact that they may wander onto your homestead. This can indeed cause panic, but I implore you to keep your wits about you. You can learn to coexist with animal wildlife. In fact, living in peace with these creatures is the better alternative to chasing them off. There is a lesser risk of either of you getting injured or even killed in such a circumstance. The animal's safety is just as important as your own. Remember that these types of wildlife are living where they are supposed to live. You're the outsider in this environment. Here are a few tips for keeping both you and the wildlife as safe as possible:

Get Informed

The first thing you must do to ensure your mutual safety is to know the kinds of animals present in the area. Knowing what you are dealing with allows you to be prepared for eventual run-ins. Buy a wildlife guide of the area where you choose to live or seek help from a local who possesses the right information. This knowledge is not only important for maintaining safety but also helps educate you on protecting different species in that space. Different animal species are protected by the law and vary from state to state. You can check out the state's Department of Fish & Wildlife to get a list of such animals.

Fence up!

Ensure there is as little chance as possible for wildlife to roam onto your property by installing a sturdy fence. The details of such a shield depend on the specific types of wildlife that you may encounter. For example, you may need to install a fence with an electrical element if bears and wild pigs are animals that frequent that space. On the other hand, you must install a fence that is at least 6 feet tall if wandering deer is a concern.

Discourage animals from roaming onto your property

Don't give these animals a reason to come onto your property. These animals do not come into human spaces looking for mischief. Often, it is just a matter of them trying to locate food. It is not ideal for humans to dig through the trash for food, but this is a bounty for animals. Don't tempt them by keeping all your trash in bear-proof cans or bags. If animals sense trash on your property, they are taught that this place is a source of food, and you are likely to get repeat visits. Keeping your trash under lock and key can save you from a face-to-face encounter with wildlife, but it also saves you from having to clean up a mess.

More tips for keeping safe from wildlife include:

- Do not pet wild animals
- Don't be a medic for an injured animal.
- Keep your pets and livestock from roaming around.
- Keep the foliage and plants near your property low. Many animals like to hide and camouflage in tall grass and similar plants when hunting. Low plant life will not attract them.

Lastly, I will end this section by mentioning something you should not do, and that is poisoning, shooting at, or otherwise trying to intentionally harm the animal. Instead, focus your efforts on preventative measures that will allow you to live in harmony with these animals. Always remember that no matter the species of animal, it is important to the local ecosystem. Everything is connected in nature. One small action can have a huge ripple effect. Annoyance might push you into thinking to get rid of one small animal, but more thought will show, you are actually affecting all wildlife in that space. That animal deserves respect and a safe, peaceful space to live in, just like you are.

What to do if you encounter a wild animal

Always look out for the following wild animals and keep a safe distance from them:

- Moose
- Bear
- Elk
- Cougar
- Wolf
- Coyote
- Wild boar
- Bobcat

No doubt - they are cute from a distance, but that distance must be maintained because they are also dangerous.

Despite your best attempts, you may find yourself face-to-face with one of these animals or another that poses a physical threat to you. How you react depends on the type of animal you face. Some tactics might scare one animal away but will antagonize another. For example, the standard advice is that shouting and standing your ground will chase a wild animal away. This is likely true if you encounter a small coyote or a bobcat. The situation is altogether different if you're up against a moose or bear. They might become aggressive because of your actions.

Luckily, you don't need to stock up on techniques to deal with all animals you might encounter. This is another area where learning about the animals in your area is useful. With this list handy, you set about learning what to do if you run across or into these animals. There is a plethora of sources you can gain this information from, like local experts, the internet, and the library.

Keeping safe from diseases

Bacteria and viruses… They are public enemy number one. They make us sick. They can kill us. They take us away from the things we love the most and steal our time. The Covid-19 pandemic showed how quickly life, as we know it and love it, can be taken away by things we can't even see or touch. We discovered that when the enemy is not visible, the damage can be great and irreversible.

But you can fight back against germs with simple habits like:

Wash your hands often

Even living off-the-grid, where you might not be in contact with many people, you need to protect yourself from bacteria and viruses. Washing your hands is the number one way to do this. Remember that sanitation, hygiene, and safety are major reasons. It is important to locate a water source and ensure your home is supplied with water before you make the move.

Using clean, warm water and anti-bacterial soap goes a long way in killing infectious and communicable diseases. Frequent hand washing stops the spread of bacteria and viruses that cause the common cold, the flu, covid-19, and more.

Clean and disinfect frequently used surfaces in your home often

Bacteria and viruses can live on your hands, and they also live on the surfaces in your home. Touching can spread germs from your hands to these often-used surfaces and vice versa. Use an antibacterial soap and water to clean them. Bleach solutions and disinfectants can also be utilized to effectively tackle these unseen enemies.

Avoid sharing personal items that cannot be disinfected

Examples include toothbrushes, razor blades, and underwear. Sharing is a great practice, but sharing germs is not categorized as being generous. That is one instance where it is better to keep it to yourself. Other people will thank you for it. Minimize the risk of spreading illnesses by using only personal items that belong to you and avoiding using anyone else's.

Do not touch wild animals

Infectious illnesses can be spread from my animals to humans. The easiest way to avoid becoming a victim is to avoid touching wild animals.

Handle and prepare food safely

Food-borne diseases can do a number on you and are often revealed by symptoms such as vomiting and diarrhea. You can protect yourself from these by doing your best to kill germs that are carried on food. Hand washing before and after you handle food is a sure way to do this. Also, thoroughly wash cooking surfaces and tools used when preparing food. Always wash your fruits and veggies before eating or using them. Cook and preserve foods at the temperatures recommended. Never eat food where you are unsure of its health repercussions.

More tips for protecting yourself from diseases

- Cough and sneeze into your sleeve instead of your hands
- Stay home and away from other people when you are sick
- Never share needles if they are used for injecting medication. One syringe or needle can only be used once.

Of course, you must keep yourself safe from illnesses that arise from pandemics, but your home can be a breeding ground for disease if you do not maintain it to a high hygienic standard.

Let's circle back to the issue of trash. They can attract local wildlife like coyotes and bears. We tend to shrug off such an occurrence because we note that these animals play a vital role in sustaining the local ecosystem. We may even be tolerant of smaller animals like raccoons. But most of us instantly cringe at rats coming onto our property. Let's make it clear off the bat. These creatures do also play a role in the local ecosystem. However, that role needs to be played out there and not in your home.

Rats and mice spread over 30 diseases with the pitter-patter of their tiny feet. This does not just occur through directly handling rats or even getting bitten by one. It also happens through contact with the rodent's urine or feces. These rodents are attracted to trash. The kicker is that once they sense that avenue to getting food, they instantly settle in, and getting rid of them is a headache. Rats account for millions of dollars in property damage every year by diminishing the home structure, chewing through electrical components, and more. These activities can lead to fires, destroying the home that you have worked so hard to build.

Trash breeds illness. Luckily, you can keep your premises clean with basic steps that ensure health and safety for yourself and your family. A proper waste management system is relatively easy to install. Use different bins for different purposes, such as having separate bins for recycling and organic waste. Reduce the amount of food waste you have. Do not keep trash in plastic bags and dispose of it promptly and responsibly.

Of course, the goal is to keep rats away, but you must know the signs of an infestation. Seeing one creature is a sure sign that cannot be ignored. The time that you see the rat can show how bad this infestation is. Rats are more active at night, and the sight of one in the daytime is a huge red flag. They are active during that time because their nest is crowded with others.

Other signs of a rat infestation include:

- Rat droppings and urine stains
- Gnawed holes serve as rat runways
- Greasy streaks on the walls

Proper sanitation prevents not only rats from invading your home but also helps get rid of an infestation. Other ways to eliminate an infestation include:

- Ensuring that there is no nesting material for these animals to set up shop in
- Removing junk piles, debris, and trash from around your home
- Keeping vegetation short and maintaining at least 3 feet of space between your home and taller plant life like bushes and shrubs
- Using rodent-proof containers to store your food and other supplies
- Install rat bats and traps
- Get a cat

Not only will these practices deter rats but also pets.

Pets can also be the cause of why you or your family get sick. If you can't keep them in a pet house outside, be sure to give them regular baths. Ensure that you have a first aid kit to deal with any sickness or injuries the pet might sustain. Do not mix this first aid kit with your own.

Other practices that keep you safe from diseases include:

- Keep your hands clean, always. Wash your hands with antibacterial soap and clean, running water as often as possible to get rid of any pathogens that might have gotten stuck on there as you touch things during your day. If water is not available, use hand sanitizer.

- Store clean water for emergencies to maintain proper hygiene even if your main water supply is cut off.
- Carry a hygiene kit. This kit contains items like paper towels, hand sanitizer, soaps, and toothpaste. They allow you to maintain good hygiene no matter where you are.
- Use a dustbin to pick up stray pieces as you clean your home. Even the tiniest particle of dust can carry bacteria that cause your entire household to be sick.

Keeping safe from harsh weather

Mother Nature is beautiful, indeed a vessel for benevolence and care. But she can also be frightening with her intensity. She has a way of testing your resilience. She knows the suitable recipes to whip up a testing ground for survival.

We create and innovate bigger and more robust buildings. We "weather-proof" this structure for the environment. The weather monitoring systems we develop are becoming more accurate. These activities and more have given us a sense of comfort. And so, we have gotten complacent about the weather conditions. That holds steady mostly. But extremes can occur at any time. No matter how big or tall the earthquake-proof, hurricane-proof... or any other design element we incorporate, nature is the strongest force you will ever encounter. She can make any of these characteristics void in no time at all. We often fear things that are evidenced, like a bear being right in front of us. However, facing the wrath of a full-grown angry bear is nothing compared to the wrath of Mother Nature, apparent in extreme weather.

But the great thing about these tests is that you still have hope of passing... once you prepare for those tests. Learn how to protect your home, farm, and livestock from harsh winters, scorching summers, and more with the following activities:

Protect your poultry and livestock by keeping them in a dry shelter

They deserve the same care, and consideration humans do in times of crisis. They depend on you for that care, so ensure they are always safe. Some animals do better in colder weather, while the opposite is true for other animals. Ensure that you choose the right livestock for that climate to ensure the best chances of survival during extreme weather conditions.

Larger animals like horses and cattle can make it through extreme weather if water is nearby. However, as conditions worsen, a warm, dry barn is needed to house these animals. Smaller animals like chickens must be provided with a dry shelter where drafts are absent.

Practice winter safety

This section is specifically for off-gridders in cold climates. Care for yourself and your family during blizzard conditions with these preparation tips:

- Be informed about the weather forecast and listen for when wind chills are expected
- Keep extra winter clothes and gear on hand and have them ready to put on at a moment's notice
- Choose the right shoes for winter. The soles must have good traction. When in doubt, snow boots or hiking boots work best for winter conditions
- Ensure your chimneys and fireplaces are clean
- Stack up enough firewood if you have a fireplace or wood stove
- Ensure your heating system is working optimally
- Keep your vehicles clean of snow and ice
- Ensure your tires are all-weather or snow tires

- Ensure that your gas tank has been filled to prevent ice from getting into the fuel lines and tank
- Keep an emergency kit in your vehicle that includes items like water, a first aid kit, snacks, blankets, flashlights, a portable cell phone charger, emergency flares, and extra batteries.
- Keep a similar kit in your home
- Place wintertime fluid in your windshield washer.
- Keep pathways shoveled or plowed free of snow
- Only shovel fresh, powder-like snow as it is lighter
- When shoveling, stretch before you begin and start slowly. Do not overexert yourself.
- Push when shoveling snow rather than lift it. If lifting is required, use a small shovel, or only partially fill a bigger shovel. Lift with your legs rather than your back.
- Prepare for de-freezing water in winter

Always have some basic tools at your disposal

This list includes knives, tarps, bedding, heater, and candles. The right tools can mean the difference between life and death. Assess which weather phenomena are most likely to occur in your area. Even if the likelihood is low, ensure you are prepared for it with the right tools close by. Some essential tools help in almost any emergency, such as those listed above. Ensure you have these stocked.

Protect your plants from the scorching heat

Do so by:

- Ensuring proper water supply
- Water regularly but do not over water the plants.
- Water the plants first thing in the morning, as this better prepares the plants to take the heat stress of the coming day
- Do not water the plants overhead as water the leaves cue sunlight to reflect off them, causing burning
- Use mulch to reduce evaporation from the soil and to conserve water as you will have to water the plants less

Chapter Summary

Keeping safe off-the-grid is not just about protecting yourself from other human beings and natural and manmade disasters. You must develop the know-how and skills for protecting yourself from wildlife, diseases, and localized harsh weather.

AFTERWORD

Life is meant to be lived as an adventure. We are meant to see new things and experience new things. We are meant to be soothed by the sounds, sights and feel of nature. We are not meant to stare at concrete and inhale toxic smog day in and day out. Instead, being able to take a deep breath of clean air is our purpose. We are not meant to slave away at 9 to 5s that we hate. We are meant to explore and nourish our souls with the seed's nature plants in every single corner of this planet. Being caged to a life where the cost of living is like a noose around your neck kills. Your heart and soul perish, and your body follows, maybe slowly but surely.

But there is an alternative. You can unplug from the grid, the thing that ties so many to a life that is survived and not thrived, and free yourself like a bird that finally takes flight. Off-the-grid living gives you those wings.

There are many falsehoods spread about this lifestyle, but you can be assured that the only truth pertaining to living off-the-grid is disconnecting from the typical electricity utility. Everything else is customizable. You choose the location where you live. You choose the type of home that fits your needs and wants best. You choose the other utilities that you stay connected to and which you become independent of. You choose which activities like gardening, foraging and livestock raising, that supplement that self-sufficiency. Off-the-grid living is what you want it to be and what you make it.

With different thoughts and opinions being voiced about off-the-grid living (both negative and positive), it is understandable if you have been on the fence about making the shift. This book was written to take all those voices out of your ear and give you the facts. Even if you had decided that off-gridding is the way forward for you, you may have felt intimidated by the process and regulations surrounding making that lifestyle your reality. The pages before were created to lift the veil that obscures the planning, designing, and building of a homestead that you can be proud to call your own. We have outlined how to do this sustainably and on any budget. Of course, there is an investment required to make this dream come true but being an off-gridder is not out of reach even if you don't have a great deal of funding.

It does take a good amount of effort, especially up front. There is no doubt about that. But neither is it as hard as it is often made out to be. Once you have committed to continuously educating yourself about the components necessary for removing yourself from modern living norms, you can do anything.

I applaud you for reading this book in its entirety. It shows your commitment to cutting the cord that ties you to mediocre living. It shows that you are ready to suckle from Mother Nature's bosom and plant roots in the great beyond. It shows that you are taking those steps that lead you to freedom.

I did it. My brother has done it. You can do it, too. Just take one step at a time.

The thrill of exploring an uncharted territory... There is nothing like it. Those feelings only grow bigger and better when you are skilled in the right way, and you have the right tools. This guide gives you what you need! Take it as your companion as you explore the many wonders the world has to offer. Refer to it time and time again if needed as you try your hand at sustainable living!

Help someone else who longs to break free from the rat race by leaving a review of your experience reading this book. May your words reach the people who need them most.

Good luck with your off-the-grid journey!

BIBLIOGRAPHY

13 places in America where land is free and owning a home is actually possible. (2022, May 9). Retrieved from https://www.point2homes.com/news/us-real-estate-news/13-places-in-america-where-land-is-free-and-owning-a-home-is-actually-possible.html

13 places in the US where you can find free land for your homestead. (2019, November 13). Retrieved from https://morningchores.com/free-land/

Aro, J. (2021, November 3). The benefits of living off the grid. Retrieved from https://medium.com/realmoneygoals/the-benefits-of-living-off-the-grid-b0bb8b59fe3d

How to build a dirt-cheap, off-grid house. (2014, July 14). Retrieved from https://www.offthegridnews.com/how-to-2/how-to-build-a-dirt-cheap-off-grid-house/

Living off-the-gridin the USA – Is it illegal? (2022, June 27). Retrieved from https://www.thesmartsurvivalist.com/living-off-the-grid-in-the-usa-is-it-illegal/

Off grid living legal states 2022. (n.d.). Retrieved from https://world populationreview.com/state-rankings/off-grid-living-legal-states

Schwartz, D. M. (n.d.). Best states to live off grid: All 50 states ranked. Retrieved from https://offgridpermaculture.com/Finding_Land/Best_States_to_Live_Off_Grid__All_50_States_Ranked.html

Victoria. (2019, April 4). 7 common misconceptions of living off the grid. Retrieved from https://www.amodernhomestead.com/misconceptions-living-off-the-grid/

Victoria. (2019, March 16). Living off the grid: 7 challenges and how to overcome them. Retrieved from https://www.amodernhomestead.com/living-off-the-grid-challenges/

Where is the best place to live off-the-gridin the USA? (2022, June 27). Retrieved from https://www.thesmartsurvivalist.com/where-is-the-best-place-to-live-off-the-grid-in-the-usa/

Made in United States
North Haven, CT
08 April 2023

35196061R00117